T0284933

# LOSS,
# A LOVE
# STORY

# LOSS, A LOVE STORY

## IMAGINED HISTORIES AND BRIEF ENCOUNTERS

## SOPHIE RATCLIFFE

NORTHWESTERN UNIVERSITY PRESS
EVANSTON, ILLINOIS

Northwestern University Press
www.nupress.northwestern.edu

An earlier version of this book was published under the title
*The Lost Properties of Love: An Exhibition of Myself*
by William Collins, London, in 2019.

This book contains many literary allusions, which are
attributed on page 203, "Sources of Quotations."

Printed in the United States of America

10   9   8   7   6   5   4   3   2   1

Library of Congress Cataloging-in-Publication Data

Names: Ratcliffe, Sophie, 1975– author.
Title: Loss, a love story : imagined histories and brief encounters / Sophie
Ratcliffe.
Other titles: Lost properties of love
Description: Evanston, Illinois : Northwestern University Press, 2024. |
"An earlier version of this book was published under the title The Lost
Properties of Love: An Exhibition of Myself by William Collins, London,
in 2019"— title page verso.
Identifiers: LCCN 2023051920 | ISBN 9780810146822 (cloth) | ISBN
9780810146839 (ebook)
Subjects: LCSH: Ratcliffe, Sophie, 1975– Family. | Tolstoy, Leo, graf,
1828–1910. Anna Karenina—Influence. | Karenina, Anna (Fictitious
character) | Loss (Psychology) | Families. | Marriage. | Marriage in literature.
Classification: LCC HQ519 .R376 2024 | DDC 155.9/3—dc23/eng/20231201
LC record available at https://lccn.loc.gov/2023051920

**AUTHOR'S NOTE**

Though not an autobiography, this book contains an account of my life. Small details have been changed to protect the privacy of others. I have also played the biographer, reimagined other people's imaginings, conjectured alternative lives, and wandered into fiction. It is an exhibition of kinds.

Oxford, September 2023

# CONTENTS

# DEPARTURES

## —1988—

DEATH, FOR ME, SMELLS LIKE SUMMER AND COMMODES, and sounds like pop.

It was September of 1988, and I'd already spent most of the holidays in my bedroom with my purple radio cassette player, waiting for my father to die. Guns N' Roses were slipping back down the charts, and the highest climber was Jason Donovan with "Nothing Can Divide Us." Kylie Minogue and Belinda Carlisle and Big Fun had a strong showing. I clung to the upbeat of Yazz and the Plastic Population and the sunshine mix of Bill Withers. By the time school started, nothing had changed. I had a flute exam coming up. New in at No. 37 was "Revolution Baby" from Transvision Vamp. He was still dying. Anthrax had gone down a spot with "Make Me Laugh."

I was woken by a noise. I could tell from the volume that my mother was standing somewhere near the airing cupboard, the one with the copper cistern wrapped in a red life jacket. The baby, my sister, started crying, too. I got out of bed. As a short, flat-chested thirteen-year-old with unfeasibly large feet, I spent a great deal of time thinking that I had nothing to wear. But that particular morning, I felt it more distinctly than usual. Neither *Just Seventeen* nor *Good Housekeeping*'s "A Look for a Lifestyle" had covered the matter of what to wear on the day your father dies—painfully and messily, before his time—when you have a day of corpse viewing ahead of you.

In the end, I put on the skirt that I wore for choir, with panels that swirled on the bias, a three-quarter-length navy

I

sweatshirt with an ersatz-Victorian plasticized picture of a floral bouquet on it, and my best electric-blue loafers. The black tights were a mistake. It was going to be, as Bill said, a lovely day.

# HULL TO FERRIBY

## —2016—

I AM SITTING AT THE BACK OF THE TRAIN, NEAR THE LOO, 280 minutes from home. For the next few hours I will look out of the window at Gilberdyke and Goole and Derby and nobody will sit on my lap. As we move, I can see the edges of Paragon land, the scrubby waste and half-slant new builds, and the warehouses and lorry parks around Hessle Road.

You knew this landscape well.

There's a moment, today, where our lines will cross. I know you're out there, as I make my way south. Out there, hanging in there. Longitudes. I press a hand against the glass and look at the imprint—a trace map. The acres of purple sky and scrap metal give way to green. This is as close as I can get.

It began as a game. I was single, in my best coat, with half a job. You were married and owned the room. Lanyarded, we stood at the conference buffet, spiking mini fish balls on cocktail sticks. I asked if I could write to you. For work. An interview about your last exhibition. You looked at my face and I could see. Something crossed your mind. You wrote your number down in my notebook, and you wished me luck. I played it cool to start with, even with myself. I kept losing the notebook, as if it were all down to luck. If it turned up, I would call. I could let chance choose if we ever met again. And then I phoned. After that, it was you who called most, and we spoke late into the night. Soon, I knew where you were sitting when we spoke, at your desk, with the film reels and cameras around you, and the blinds half shuttering out the gray city air. Once you wrote down the other number, with instructions about when I could use it and when I must destroy it. The betrayal of your other life—your betrayal, my complicity, our betrayal—was something I rarely felt, but then it struck me clearly in the surprisingly delicate precision of your light blue Biro.

You used to call me and stay on the line for ages, sometimes so quiet that we could hear each other breathe. I've never liked phone calls. I do not like the act of dialing, the being called. But with you I didn't mind. It was one of our ways of being together. Being on the line. There was no line of course.

I still dream about you. We are at a Christmas party. In a lift. Eating a pizza on a bench in Battersea. (We are an unlikely couple, even in dream world.) An older man with a camera bag and a newspaper. A not young, but younger, woman, wearing a leopard-print top. I wake and hope to dream again.

It's nine years since I've seen your face. Or heard your voice. I don't have either of your numbers anymore, and if I did, I wouldn't call. But the other day I tried to find you again, circling the streets of your city on my computer screen in a 360-degree spin. Then closer up, zooming in on the house numbers as if I might, if I looked hard enough, catch sight of you through the window, walking away.

Not that your face was much to write home about. Not that I could write home about it in any case. Happily married women don't write home about other men's faces.

There's a flash of names beneath the bindweed. *Shipham Valves. Wan Hai. Atlas Leisure Homes.* Then leveling out to follow the motorway, chasing the cars past the Humber.

The light changes, turns brighter, over the stretch of brown with its drag of sand. I open my handbag to look for my book. In a week, my students will get back, and my lectures are still unwritten. They'll have their own copies of different books, and most will remember to bring them. Some of these books will be well read, well thumbed, decorated with lines of tiny Post-it notes like stiff fluorescent tongues. Others will look more like mine—almost brand new, with an uncreased spine and a shine to its cover. This is the fourth *Anna Karenina* I have bought. I have a habit of losing anything I am trying to work on, of leaving it in a cupboard or a suitcase or a plastic bag. Somewhere, back home, there are three other books like this. Each has its own cover, its own bends and creases, and corners rubbed with wear. They will turn up in the end, among piles of paperwork or under the bed. Eventually, I will group them all together on a shelf, and they will stand there, reproachful relatives, as if I should have stuck to one of them. I turn the title page. *All happy families are alike, each unhappy family is unhappy in its own way*.

That's not the real first line of course, but I have no Russian. I close the book and look out of the window. The train goes over a metal bridge with a whistling sound, then past the endless backs of houses. We are stopping and starting now, slowly enough to peer into other people's conservatories, at their laundry and sheds and swing sets and greenhouses and statues of frogs on toadstools, and upturned trampolines, then out to the fields lined with yellow rapeseed, and the crowd of wind turbines circling like alien gymnasts. I press my finger against the glass again and try to write.

*Someone I nearly loved is dying.*

5

The letters evaporate, replaced by lines of turbines, receding into the distance, gray and slim. One has got stuck mid-cycle. Its paddles seem to droop against the sky. Perhaps it can't go forward without turning back.

# ST. PETERSBURG
# TO MOSCOW

ANNA OPENS HER BOOK AND STARTS TO READ, SETTLING back on the white sprung seat nearest to the window side. She turns the pages carefully, studying the shape of the words and feeling the soft, thin paper between her fingers, then looks up and around. There is a pleasant kind of loneliness to this train world. A moment where she can ask where to be, how to be a person, when the strings of life have been loosened from around her. The others seem deep in thought. Perhaps they are loosened too. The first-class carriage seats four. Four bodies, set against a background of patterned wallpaper—two, like her, staring into the distance, lost in thought. A mobile salon. She is unencumbered, her smaller bags and trunks stowed on the luggage rail above her head, the hatbox on the top of the pile pulsing slightly to the train's rhythm. The telegraph wires disappear in the distance like broken trees, and outside the window the skeins of smoke float gently upward, then break into strands, vanishing, as if lacking the conviction to go on. The older woman opposite has finally drifted off to sleep. Anna fingers the covered seat button, feeling the pressure of compacted horsehair under the fabric. The oil lamp is growing dimmer, but still gives her enough light to read. She sips her glass of tea in its silver holder, half-conscious of the sound of the train jolting over the rails. She follows the rise and fall of the English prose.

The characters in her book walk in and out of rooms with boxes of papers. A government minister forms an alliance.

A woman called Kate rides to hounds. Anna imagines joining the ride, sitting sidesaddle in her habit, with a fur collar and dancing eyes. A proposal might happen. A frisson. Everyone is watching as they jump the fence. It would make a good picture.

Her album sits on the arm of her chair, the album she carries everywhere. Inside it is her son's portrait. Her favorite photograph, the latest one—him in a white smock, sitting backward on a chair, with frowning eyes and smiling lips. This was how he looked. It was his best, most characteristic expression, the one he brought to her when he wanted a new toy or another story at bedtime or a warm cup of milk or a song. She can only think of him with a smile. Her small love.

Tolstoy is good on details, like smiles and soup and eyes and trains. He is good on the small things—those miraculously ordinary things that make up life. He writes of the way Anna's train pulls into the station, the coupling rod of the middle wheel slowly and rhythmically turning and straightening—of the *muffled, hoarfrost-covered driver* and the *puffing steam* grazing the frozen ground. He notices the look of a luggage wagon, the sound of a little yelping dog. He writes, in a letter to his cousin, of the minute particulars of each of his children. One finds that currant jelly and buckwheat make his lips itch. Another turns his elbows out as he crawls around the kitchen floor. In the 847 pages of my paperback *Anna Karenina*, he tells us the precise color of a mushroom, the type of leather on a sofa, and the way it feels to scythe a field of grass. He knows the places people keep their slippers and their dressing gowns, the particular North Sea coast where their oysters are sourced. He knows how people worry about their faces getting wrinkles, or about sick cows, or about running out of milk. He lists the things in one man's pocket—the cigarettes, the pocketbook, the matches, and the watch with its double chain and seals. He watches someone order cabbage soup. He describes the texture of a still-damp morning paper about to be read, the pattern of hairpins clustering at the nape of a woman's neck, the little muff hanging from the cord of a skating girl's coat.

Objects mattered to Tolstoy. They spoke, saying something in their intractability, in their power. The smallest of treasures. The properties that for him constituted the whole of memory and the feeling of love. The tiny ball hanging from a nursemaid's necklace. The plaited belt of a dressing gown, hanging down at the back. A pair of handmade boots. Perhaps these things mattered to Tolstoy because he had lost so much. As a young soldier, he had taken to gambling. The debts mounted up. He wrote back to his lawyer. Sell something, he said. The lawyer sold his house. Yasnaya Polyana. It means Bright Glade. When Tolstoy got back, they'd dismantled most of it. He was left with a hole in the ground.

He made his home in the little that remained and built on it. A new Bright Glade, next to the old, in the countryside southwest of Tula. There is a whole room at Yasnaya Polyana devoted to his stuff, ranged behind the cabinets, stacked carefully in tissue-paper-lined chests. You can see it all there—and more of it in his Moscow house. His music collection and his handmade shirts. His bicycle and dumbbells. On his desk, under a glass box, there are two brass candlesticks. Three inkwells are ranged on a stand. A small brass dog and a paperweight sit beside a tarnished silver pot of quills. His writing chair is low, legs sawn down so that he could get closer to the paper as his eyesight failed.

Tolstoy needed to be close to things. Art, for him, begins with the smallest of differences: where *minute and infinitesimally small* changes occur. Real life is not lived, he wrote in the big stories. Truth is not where people fight, and slay one another. Life is in the between-ness, the space in the margins. It is in the brokenness of everyday things. Every one of the changes in the world comes to pass, and comes to be felt, through the pulse of our lives, through the smallest of happenings. We exist and make our way to our own truth in the same small fundamental movements, around the tiny portions of our own lives.

Tolstoy cared about the details you couldn't touch, too. Details like a mood, or a blush, or a silence. Details like time. Nabokov said that Tolstoy was the only writer whose *watch keeps time with the numberless watches of his readers*. His prose *keeps pace with our pulses*. He knew slow time. The time it takes for two men to choose their dinner in a Russian-French restaurant. The time it takes to adjust a hat in a hallway mirror. The timing of a pause in conversation, when one person attempts to bring up a difficult subject, and the hesitation as the other looks away. The way time hangs heavy for those in love.

Anna's time is governed by others. She is a moving character, forever coming and going, subject to other people's clocks, never quite at home. *"Every heart has its own skeletons," as the English say.* This time, this now, she is on a visit to her brother in Moscow, leaving her own family, her husband and son, in St. Petersburg. As it draws toward six o'clock, the sky turns from pearly gray to black. She sees the frosted conifers from the window, dark bottle-green. The ground is a white blanket, with patches of rough grass pushing up through the snowy verge like so many undone chores.

Across the aisle, a woman is reading a magazine article about the wonders of river cruising, eating a Kinder Bueno. Her T-shirt says something about love in curly writing. Her neighbor is folding up a small kite and putting it into her rucksack. A man stands, leaning against the seat as he checks his phone. Looking down the aisle, I see a row of elbows receding into the distance, with a mess of bag straps hanging down from the overhead shelf. Wi-Fi is not available.

As we speed up past the drainage canals and conservatories filled with cactuses, I see a station appear and disappear too quickly for me to read the name, the letters blurring to a streak on the sign placed in a stretch of rainy-day concrete. It was somewhere. The unreadable somewheres. Those are the lost places, the ones I never get to or, at least, never get off at. You can see them down the timetable. Hessle, Ferriby, Broomfleet, Thorne North. It's one of them there, vanishing into the distance like a half-grasped memory. But the sense of loss, the feeling that you might have left something behind in the cloakroom, is displaced by the reassuring forward movement of the train.

For a moment, we all travel at the same speed. Or are stationary together. Nonstop services give you this feeling more strongly. On a train, perhaps more intensely than on any other form of transport, our spatial and temporal responsibility is gone, our destination preordained.

It's just an illusion, of course. The train driver could suddenly decide that she wanted to stop. The train could break. It could blow up. I could jump out of the window. We could crash. It's happened. One Valentine's Day morning in 1927, the incoming 7:22 from Withernsea smashed into the 9:05 to Scarborough. The British Pathé footage shows ten men in bowler hats and raincoats inspecting the wreckage; the smoke from their cigarettes rises in spirals against the mist. A front engine is half-telescoped, a carriage smashed, open to the air. Trains are driven by people, not machines, and that Valentine's Day one person pulled the wrong signal lever. First nine dead. Then twelve. Human error.

My train is a safe place. I cannot be lost. The lady cannot vanish, except by a kind of illusion. The trajectory is set, and, as we power forward, we look into something like a fixed future. Time is out of my hands, and, for that reason, for now, I feel free.

I cannot hold it, or hold it up.

# HACKNEY WICK

## —2003—

HAVING LUNCH IN YOUR FLAT FOR THE FIRST TIME, I rearrange my body as I eat, trying to work out which way I should sit. Leaning in, leaning out, leaning forward on the table to express interest, then back again in the chair, my hands neatly folded. Seen through a lens, we would have made an uncomfortable picture: dimly lit, bad angles.

I wonder where I should put myself.

Your images on the walls around me have no such trouble. A large canvas propped against the left-hand wall near the doorway. Careful still lives, stacked against each other, waiting to be taken for a hanging. A picture of what I think is a plate and a jug. Sturdy and weighted. You liked to look at things and the ways they were positioned, one against another. The placement and arrangement. The spaces between.

I sit and try to work out the years between us. Over thirty, whichever way you counted. Years that meant not just time but marriage, children, money, friends—all of which were still unknown then. I was just starting out. You were just starting to retire.

After a bit, a meal of steak and salad. (I tried to look not hungry.) It was the only time I saw you cook. Strawberries for afters, but we skipped them.

# FERRIBY TO BROUGH
## —2016—

WHAT DO HAPPY FAMILIES LOOK LIKE? I THINK THROUGH the cards in the game. Mr. Bun the Baker, Mrs. Chip the Carpenter's wife, Master Soot the Sweep's son. Neat groups of four, matching sets fitting neatly into the palm of your hand.

Fitting together is harder than it looks. It's worst in the morning, as my family gropes its way toward various syncopated goodbyes. At some point, during toaster and juice supervision, I run upstairs to pull on some clothes. Fishing around for a dress with no waist, and a pair of earrings, then hunting through the dirty-clothes basket for a pair of tights and finding some with a (painfully constricting) hole in the toe. I make my way to the front door, tripping over assorted shoes and a collapsing toy pram. My son stands by the front gate and asks if he can play Minecraft. I wonder when I last took the time to comb his hair. To read him a book. How much time is it fair to take? How much belongs to me? The question wheels in my mind, like a foot in midair, between platform and rails. I want to fall.

*No more sombre enemy of good art than the pram in the hall.* So said Cyril Connolly. This is a fundamental misunderstanding of childcare equipment. With a pram there's movement. A pram-pusher can think, walk, and carry baggage. And there's a chance that the pram's occupant might go to sleep. Prams don't even have to be taken out for an airing. They can be rocked up and down a hallway with a laptop in the hood and a paragraph has a possibility of being born. Other things get in the way of art. Laundry. The school run. Plates of food that always seem to need clearing away. The clutter on the living room floor. The tidying up, and the nits, and the compromise. These are the things that get in the way. Along with the bills and the boiler maintenance. The train set's wooden circle, its level crossings, its half-built bridge. The half-eaten fish finger on the plastic plate (not mine).

It is quiet right now, apart from the sound of engine against track, that familiar juddering, grinding, and groaning of metal. Out of the window to my right, the fields, cut across with drainage canals, lakes and spinneys and car parks and Portakabins. I look at the bag of books and papers beside me. This, if I'm lucky, is the beginning of the middle of my life. It is a time when promising thirtysomething starts to give way to middling fortysomething—a strange in-between period where horizons and trousers shrink. My nights are spent chasing not men but lost PE kit. Middles can be hard to navigate: we never know exactly where they begin. How should we pace ourselves? Is there a schedule? I scroll through the mental calendar. Ghosts are planted on various pages, next to bank holidays and festivals. My dead teacher. My dead friend. Back to my father. Dead at forty-five, he hovers over each September, a corduroy shade, condemned to perpetual middle age. I imagine the ghost you will soon be.

I am alone in my carriage, with the fifty-six other passengers. Alone together, moving to the same rhythm. I pull my phone out. There are squares and squares of photographs that contract at the touch of the screen, disappearing into tessellated blocks, a mosaic of motherhood. One of a parent's first instincts, one of the first things they do once a child enters their life, is to begin to capture it. To render it still and permanent. As children grow, the photo album, or the ever-present camera phone, is like a talisman. We photograph our children a thousand times. To pin them down, as if the recording might render them ours forever, ever more perfect, but never more perfect. Photographs: the only place where things can last, as the gaze from the screen stares out of time. An illusion. It's where we outsource our lament against time's passing. Where we park our fear of death. White borders contain it all. Nothing must be lost.

The man on the other side of the aisle is writing an email and the woman in front of me is staring at a spreadsheet. My phone is about to die, but I can still look at pictures of my children, for now. And later, I will still picture them, like negatives, the pair of them shuttering across the back of my mind with a wave of impossible love. There they are—still—hanging upside down off the rails near the park, laughing with open mouths. Squinting into the sun beside a beach hut. Holding ice creams in hands that are small.

# ST. PETERSBURG
# TO MOSCOW

ANNA TURNS ANOTHER PAGE OF HER ENGLISH NOVEL.
The woman who has been out riding is now writing an
imaginary letter, then putting an imaginary hat on, before
walking out of the door for the imaginary station. What
Anna reads is make-believe, but that's her substance too.
She is a chimera, pure fiction. Not that there's anything
pure about fiction. Anna is pieced together, as we all are, by
fragments of others, imaginary and real. She is a combination. A blend. An infusion of people whom Tolstoy had met,
or missed. Of things that he'd read, or imagined his heroine
might have read. Open her up, case by case, like a matryo-
shka doll, and the selves reveal themselves. Line them up,
an identity parade.

One of the dolls is slightly out of line. She refuses to fit.
She wants to escape to another story, to break the case and
start her own. Her name is Kate Field, and she was a journalist, lecturer, and early telephone pioneer. Her thousands of
articles—like the people she wrote for—are just a blur on the
literary timeline, almost out of view. She is a real woman lost
in time. A detail I cannot let go.

Kate Field wasn't Tolstoy's muse, not even in the loosest
sense of the word. He probably didn't even know she existed.
But in the way that one late train can upset the entire South
Western train service, Kate Field made an impression on
Tolstoy's world.

I know the beginning. Not the first day, first hour, first moment, but the general time and place. It began in Florence, where she first met a man with steady eyes and a way of watching the world. Anthony Trollope was forty-four and married. Kate Field was twenty-one and got under his skin. Gifts were exchanged (a copy of *The Arabian Nights*). And letters. And then they all went home.

But gradually, quietly, the Field of Trollope's imagination entered his fiction. He wrote to her, and began to write about her. Numerous versions of Field haunt his novels. Different sorts of women, all a bit like Field, often called Kate, trail their way through the pages of his books. Books that found themselves printed and reprinted, imported and placed in bookshops in Paris and Berlin, Moscow and St. Petersburg.

Whenever Tolstoy readied himself to write, he turned to reading English novels. And this is how Kate Field found her way to him, with the make-believe of a beginning. Sitting in Yasnaya Polyana, Tolstoy read about these women, these imaginary Kate Fields. And he loved them. He lined the books up on his shelf. He remembered them. They crept into his mind, and into his work.

Parts of Kate Field live on in Anna Karenina. Anna Karenina is partly Kate Field. That's what writers do. They change lives.

# HACKNEY WICK

## —2005—

A HOT AUGUST MORNING AND WE LAY ON TOP OF THE bedsheets in a pile of body. You got up to take a call and I looked at my legs on the whiteness.

*Summer in the city.*

Outside the window, a bird settled on the nearby guttering.

It was as free as.

Double portraits are always the hardest, you said as you walked back in. The lens has to settle for something. It has to choose one thing or another. An eye. A coat button. A parakeet.

# BATTERY PLACE TO CORTLANDT STREET

DISTANCE WAS KATE FIELD'S STYLE. WALKING DOWN BROAD-way, taking her time as she crossed over to Fulton and then left again down Greenwich. Rain was promised, and few would have been tramping the usually crowded sidewalks, as the sky above Lower Manhattan turned dark gray. Then stopping at the Friend Pitts store near Amity Street (now West Third) to pick up a precautionary umbrella. Down to the intersection of Cortlandt and Greenwich Streets.

She'd just been framed—a picture with Anthony—and now she was trying to get away. She was always trying to get away. Her life was a series of broken connections, a shimmering circle, closed on the outside. The sitting had taken an age. They could have gone to any one of the quicker Broadway studios. Fredericks' Photographic Temple opposite the Metropolitan, or to Gurney's, farther down. But Napoleon Sarony at 680 was the go-to. He could render the impression of something coming into relief, almost stepping out of the paper. His figures were all life and expression. No stiff jaws and staring eyes for him, none of those brocade drapes and sad ferns. Sarony made a body seem in motion, even while that body was caught in an iron head brace, waiting for twenty seconds or more, not moving. He was an illusionist, playing with time. Slow motion looked fast. Still looked like moving.

She was glad not to be near all those people anymore, to leave the cluttered studio. A large alligator hung from the ceiling of his waiting room. Greek busts and tapestries jostled for space with stuffed birds and lampstands shaped like Buddhas. The studio itself was stark and strange—full of glare and bareness, metal posing frames. The smell of ether and lavender oil, asphalt and sandarac gum, of dragon's blood. The photograph of the pair hasn't survived. Lost, or destroyed, perhaps. Broken, maybe. But what would it have told us anyway? Feeling is what we lose in time. The feeling that lies between. The tension or the frisson. The flirtation, or unrequited love. There is no earthly way to record the thing that never happened, even if two people know how nearly it did. What makes someone walk into someone else's marriage, or out of their own? What makes someone end a relationship, or a life, placing their foot into the future's thin air? What makes someone start an affair?

People talk. They say Trollope and Field were in love— or, at least, that he loved her, or almost loved her. They say his wife knew, or was vexed by it. They read between the lines of his novels. Tell us that he never got over her. The photographs we have tell us something, and nothing. If the camera never lies, then the photos that remain show two separate people, neither of them gazing into the lens, nor looking in quite the same direction. Trollope sits straightforwardly, angled just a little away from center, as if he is about to say something to someone. His eyes look directly at the viewer through his metal spectacles, his enormous beard runs from the top of his ears out toward the camera. Her eyes are set at a middle-distance dream, her face and shoulders a quarter turn from the camera lens. Her hair looks fine. Caught before the rain began. Appearances mattered to Field. She was flamboyant. Camp, even. Hopeful that rules can be bent.

Down the studio corridor, things are developing. Two men stand, side by side, by candlelight, next to a running-water bath. One of them holds the tin sheet on his left hand, balanced like a chalice, his wrist tense with concentration. The other man passes him a small cup of developer. He flows it over the plate, timing his movements by tapping his right hand on his thigh. The lightest points appear first. Fifteen seconds in near darkness. Then the tones. The shadows come last. Surfaces and depths. The assistant leans closer to the other to check the image, looking at the levels. Then he begins to wash the plate with water, pouring the jug he has at the ready. Gently, for nothing yet is fixed. And so the surfaces of the glass transform, changing their nature. Silver nitrate and ferrous sulfate. A chemical's properties reveal themselves in change. Action and reaction. Combustion, explosion, evaporation, smoke.

Any photograph like this contains an element of risk. An ethereal solution of pyroxylin. The risk of taking too long to make a pose, or not long enough. The risk of moving during the exposure and blurring the image. And then behind the scenes, the scurry to develop the plate, the assistant holding the glass like a delicate tray. Of clumsily flowing the developing fluid or leaving it too long, and turning it black. Of scorching the image in candlelight. This picture records all those risks, and some of a less technical kind. Through the cyanide, an affair was coming into focus. Someone was nearly getting burned.

It was done. The photograph was taken, and it was time to go. Beside them, a stagecoach draws up. An unknown woman in dark red velvet is handed down from the carriage. An unknown man takes her by the arm, an intimacy legible in the way they touch. The two unknowns disappear. Trollope and Field shake hands on the sidewalk outside the marble building, as the clouds break and they ready themselves to part.

Knowingly. This goodbye might, they thought, have been their last meeting, certainly for years. It could have been forever. *The last word is not said*—probably never shall be said. Field's diaries speak of being sick at heart. She is angry with herself for wasting time. She had nobody, she wrote, to spur her into new fields. Looking on, a passerby would not have guessed that something was going on. They couldn't have seen the lines of a future absence taking shape between the two of them, the imagined distance starting to solidify.

I like to think that Trollope watched her, as she turned left. Nothing now remains of that part of Cortlandt Street. It was half flattened out for the building of the World Trade Center, then flattened again one September morning, seen now only in film clips of gray and yellow horror. She was drawn by the pictures she'd seen in the papers of iron legs, the idea of newly fragile structures hovering over the streets of Lower Manhattan. The El train. A city on the move. In her head, she'd make a sketch of mechanical speed with words, thinking through the violence of the drop, the idea of the small cars catching and releasing the iron hooks above them, like gymnasts on rings. They'd finished constructing the final sections of the railway by then. The fixed iron posts punctuated the roadways supporting the car rails, all acrobatic, airy, and perched-up. It was gray but hot, waiting to break into rain.

Beyond Peter Henderson's, men were smoking outside the Northern Hotel. She found someone from the railway company who let her climb the stairs to view an empty car. There she sat, right up on the rails, beside the second-floor windows of the dry goods stores, looking on at the passersby. She was glad for that brolly, as the rain began in earnest. Pouring down in pitchforks and then buckets onto the sidewalk. I think of you, as she thinks of him, still fading.

# BROUGH TO GOOLE

## —2016—

A MAN SLEEPS OPPOSITE ME, HIS HEAD LISTING TO THE left. An inflatable navy-blue suedette pillow matches the navy-and-silver seat velour. We go through a cutting, into the dark, then out again, past the lines of Heron Foods vans and the Emon Spice Lounge and the fields of hay cut short.

I think back to the photographs of Field. Even at a slant, her eyes look too pale to be true—almost luminously so. Another trick of the light. Collodion does not recognize the existence of blue. There was no way to catch her eyes.

Later, when they were apart, Trollope asked Field for a photograph of her facing straight ahead, full front. He said he wanted her *natural look*. Leafing through the images of Kate Field, you'll hardly ever find it. There's one of her leaning against a pillar, as if overhearing a conversation. One leaning back on a sofa, her head cupped in her hand. One profile, with French lace. One on horseback, on her way. Only one of her looking straight at the camera, all in white, a messenger bag slung across her torso. Something about her resisted that pose. Her pictures usually show her moving toward a world elsewhere, a *profil perdu*, so very French—or glancing over her shoulder, her gaze never quite meeting yours.

Sidewalk or not, they would have said farewell some-where, somehow. We never know when the last word is said. Perhaps the last word is never said. *Can anything indeed*, Field's biographer asked, *in this part of life be ever said to be the end?* We never know when our meeting with another

25

person might be the final one. Even the most heartfelt good-byes usually have a confident belief in au revoir, a next time, a next place. But on the very fringes of our consciousness there is always the sense that this might be, if not the full stop in the conversation, then a conversation left hanging. For some, the finality is always that bit closer. The hurried quality of lovers parting bears it out. Lovers' time is carved out of real time—or stolen. It's always under threat.

Any affair is an attempt to live twice. Set into the beige wall of everyday linear time, it exists beyond a door you think nobody else has noticed. You walk past doors just like it every day. Often you don't even think to look at it. But now and again, you stand beside it. You might be the sort to push open that door. Sometimes it resists your touch, or bounces gently on the hinges before shutting, and you return to the beige world. You read a safety notice about fire drills on the wall, check your phone, or fish something from your bag, as if pretending that you never even tried to push. But sometimes you are standing nearby and that door swings open seemingly of its own accord, offering a floodlit view down a pathway of nylon grass. The walk seems impossibly short. And while you are there, you have two lives, and two heartbeats. You make believe that you have created a sort of a time pocket or vortex, a duplicate self. There's something almost impossible about this other, Narnian universe. And while you are in it, nobody does it better. The moment you take your first step, you feel as if time has warped and split.

If photographs are a way of stopping time—their stilled presence, wet collodion and albumen transformed into something brittle, calm, and dry—then affairs create a negative imprint, a second life. If a camera is a *clock for seeing*, then an affair is a clock for living. For anyone hungry for time, this door is the one to open for that oh-so-dangerous illusion, the illusion of more time, more space. Of more.

Trollope always hungered. He wanted to split into pieces, to live many lives. His characters multiply, revolving, double, inconsistent. An affair with words. You can see it right from the beginning. *Please, sir, I want.* First as a bullied child walking through the streets of Harrow, dreaming of castles in the air. Then, as an adult, sitting at his desk every day. He squeezed time, waking in the dark and writing into sunrise, spooling out a thousand words an hour between five and eight in the morning. Two hundred and fifty words every fifteen minutes. *I attribute the power of doing this altogether*, he wrote, *to the virtue of early hours. It was my practice to be at my table every morning at 5:30 a.m.* His groom got up first and made him coffee, then the real day began.

Trollope logged his life in grids. Targets met or missed, days of idleness or productivity. Late one night he writes to Field, asking her to meet him at Niagara Falls, the scene of so many Victorian clinches. *If you are going . . . let me know when you go.*

I look at my book. You don't need to be a writer or an actor or a lover to dream a second life, an unlived life. You don't need to have an affair. Every reader does it. In the moment we touch the cover, a second world emerges—another reality with its own rules of space and time. And good novels knock us sideways, even as they take us forward. With every story we turn the page for, we turn to feel the weight of the unlived life, the other ways we might have gone, or loved, or died. Some are unfaithful readers. A pile of books lives next to my side of the bed, gathering dust and regret. For each book that we read, there's another we don't begin. And in choosing a tale to write, or relate, there is another we cannot, or do not, speak. These small choices carry with them an accompanying sense of resistance, a gravitational pull toward the alternatives we leave behind. The mushrooms we never picked on the picnic we never went on with the person we never met. Most of us are missing something. In so many of our imaginations, there's a vision of something like a train we missed, a moment in life when we were too late, or too scared to act. Or got stuck in the queue at the sandwich shop. Some of these trains move toward lands we've lost, some pause at stations of regret. We see others pass across the landscape of our memory with a sigh of relief. They are the boredoms we escaped, the journeys we avoided. But some are so painful we can only glimpse them at night. They pass at high speed, cornering the edge of dread, taking our breath away.

# HACKNEY WICK
## —2005—

YOUR STUDIO FLAT WAS HARD TO READ. THE PLACE WAS ALL stripped back and bald, staging a bachelor existence that wasn't yours. Even the few images that you chose to hang on the walls told a story of things that liked to be single. Black-and-white stills of an old milk jug, a spoon, a silhouette of a man on an empty piazza, pulling a lonely suitcase.

All the clean lines were just an illusion. Hiding that life made sense, of course. I get the picture, now I could risk losing the same: a discreet affair keeps things discrete. But your silence got me wanting. You reminded me of one of those plaster-cast models I used to make as a child, the ones that fell into two halves. The fascination comes from looking at what's being cut off. The straight, flat back, deliciously smooth, powder dry.

One afternoon, you left me alone to go to a shoot. License to stalk into your office. I looked behind the screen, and opened your desk drawers once to see if I could find any family pictures, then shut them again, feeling guiltier than I'd thought I would. I sat back at your desk, tried out your chair. Imagined the album I would have found. Page after page of grainy squares, bearing witness to the theater of family. Your role as husband. Your place as father.

There must be a photograph of the small you, walking on a wet promenade, smiling into a lens. I wonder if that's where it began. When you were taken by the desire to capture things. Sometimes we can pin it down to a single frame. The moment we start to become who we are.

# WEST FINCHLEY TO BELSIZE PARK

## —1982—

MY FAMILY LOOKED HAPPY ENOUGH. FROM A DISTANCE, or from the photos. We lived in an ordinary suburban house, a bit like the one in which Edith Nesbit's railway children begin their lives at the turn of the twentieth century. Ours was a bit smaller. Inside, there was a big square hall with an emerald-green tiled fireplace, and a kitchen with a glass-fronted dresser and an archaic bell system that no longer worked. There were four bedrooms upstairs and a mock balcony, accessible from the main bedroom or by climbing out of a side window, where you could sit on the slatted wooden floor and smoke Camel Lights. We even had French windows, like Nesbit's children, which hooked back so that you could walk onto a crazily paved patio. The garden was long. It had a gate leading onto the local woods. There were hydrangea bushes and a rockery in the garden. An unsteady sundial with an iron pointer that you could lift up to ambush a colony of ants running in frenzied circles. A gently rotting greenhouse, in which we used to store old furniture. It was a quiet road, the silence broken by the sound of the Tube making its way down the end of the Northern Line, or our next-door neighbor trying to kill squirrels with his air rifle. The house is my earliest memory. The front door in particular.

I remember walking down the path, looking at its pale blue wood (later painted yellow) and jewel-like panels of colored glass—blue, green, and red teardrops against a grid of lead. There were row after row of houses like this in our neighborhood, all with their own individual take on topiary or pampas grass. Our road was one of the many suburban semi developments of early twentieth-century Metroland, the place with elastic borders, no beginning and no clear end. The architectural critics call these roads joyless. Phony. A kind of Neverland. Semis like these were, in 1910, bang on trend. Tudorbethan, blackened timber nailed onto the stucco, leadlights in squares or sometimes in diamonds. In the really posh bits of London, architects lovingly built houses along these lines, attempting to capture the idea of human craft in the machine age. The ones in our street were aspirational knockoffs—the rows of pseudo-artisan houses embodied that oddest of ideas: mass-produced individuality. All suburban semis are alike, but each suburban semi is alike in its own way.

Our road was a cul-de-sac. Bag End. Traffic calmed, there was nowhere to go. If you went back the way you came, farther up the junction, onto the main road, there was the North Finchley cinema complex, and Brent Cross Shopping Centre, and the open road to Little Chef. And holidays. The North Circ, and Neasden and David Lloyd Sports Centre and multiplex cinemas. Homebase and B&Q. Smooth and bland. A place that brings with it a sort of atrophy of body and mind, a numbing alikeness. This is what J. G. Ballard called the real England. And with it, he writes, comes a boredom that *can only be relieved by some sort of violent act; by taking your mail-order Kalashnikov into the nearest supermarket and letting rip.*

A century ago, Edith Nesbit had a similar, if less scary, response to Metroland. As a ritual, each evening, she would put aside her drafts of novels and make a series of models of factories and suburban houses out of brown paper. She'd then take them out to her back garden and set them on fire. It's little wonder that Nesbit soon has her railway children leave their villa, engineering the plot so that they are forced to take a cottage in the country.

Finchley in Nesbit's day was an omnibus ride from town, up through Swiss Cottage and Golders Green. A strange mixture of city and countryside, famous for its compost heaps and Barham's model dairy farm. Visitors on the omnibus would continue through Temple Fortune for their day in the country, on the edge of the city. Overlooking the presence of Simms Motor Units, they would head for the idyll on Regent's Park Road, where they could view the rows of pedigree Express dairy cows, admire the silver bottle tops, and have a scone in the adjoining tearooms. It was a stopgap. A commuter village. From Tally Ho Corner, you could take the omnibus direct to Marylebone, or pick up the train on a cross route from Finsbury Park to Edgware. But Finchley didn't join the London Underground for years. Perhaps it makes sense that the man who designed the Tube map was off the map, at least when he first drew it. When he died, nobody even knew it was his idea. Harry Beck lived just around the corner from me—a dweller in nowhere.

Nowadays, Finchley still feels more to me like a place to pass through than a destination. A few months ago, I took a journey down the road to my old house, rounding the corner past West Avenue and Lovers Walk. Everything seemed wider and larger than I recalled, but the quality of silence was still the same. The houses are the same mixture of the dark red of the late 1980s and the determined solidity of 1930s mansion flats. I walked along the undulating road, past Chestnut Row with its pollarded trees. The house at the corner of my road has been converted to a care home. Shielded by a high fence, only parts of it are visible from the street. A burgundy awning perches above its door, desperately trying to create the effect of hotel luxury. The strange combination of porticos and extensions and satellite dishes makes it feel as if it is about to fall into the road.

Ahead to the left is Lovers Walk, the shortcut up to Ballards Lane. Not much in the way of love ever happened to me there. The closest I came was being flashed at while walking back from Tesco. My road bends to the right, down a shallow hill. It seems much the same. The same green-gated park on the left-hand side. I remember the overwhelming shades of green—conifers—and the slow descent of the road down to the bottom where our house stood, still marked by the leafless silver birch, with its white trunk and electrocuted shock of narrow branches. The road was still quiet, apart from the banging of some builders a few doors up.

There was an ache about the house that I couldn't put into words but which I remembered from before. Growing up, I understood that our house was steeped in compromise. It was not quite a mistake but felt a place in which we could never truly settle. Every few months, an outing with an estate agent acted as a peculiarly ineffective kind of family therapy. We trooped around other houses, farther down the Northern Line, nearer to town. They smelled of polish or mice, or a different kind of pain. But the houses we saw, the ones without net curtains and stucco, were unaffordable. Window shopping over, we were stuck.

Sometimes there were arguments. Quiet arguments.

Voices never raised. Tension about money, I think. Holidays. A particularly vivid un-shouting match seemed to be about what shade of beige we should paint the front room, but probably wasn't. Mostly there was just a sense of things unsaid.

My father insisted on long journeys to National Trust stately homes, and I threw up in the back seat.

Once, at the end of one weekend, something happened. Someone was not able to talk. Someone else was angry. The contents of a coffee cup were poured around the kitchen table, like a bizarre midsummer rite. We were packed into the car with suitcases. We drove to my friend's house where we arrived without warning and were awkwardly made lunch. Our suitcases remained in the hall. When we returned home and walked back into our kitchen, accomplices of this short, failed separation, my father was still standing in front of the square window above the draining board, staring at the revolving washing line and fiddling with the silver tankard full of screwdrivers, as if he'd been there all day. The magic coffee circle had been cleaned up. I watched the raindrops make their way down the glass, breaking off and then joining one another, like companionable tears. Then I went outside and played with the tap, pressing my hand against the pattern of small shiny stones embedded in concrete until it hurt. Nobody felt at home, and there was no hope of anyone going anywhere.

My father was invisibly sick. We all knew he was sick, but I didn't fully understand why or how or where. Sometimes he was at work, leaving every morning in a suit with a briefcase to do things that had something to do with the Government. Sometimes he left a little later, with a vinyl suitcase packed with pale blue pajamas, and then he was going to the Big Hospital, and didn't come back for a while. Once he was there for a very long time. We visited. The Big Hospital corridors unfurled like a medical version of Oz, rising and falling as we walked. Everything smelled of oranges and Pine Harpic. I was allowed to buy a Beatrix Potter cookery book *and* a stained-glass coloring book on the way home. Then my aunt arrived with a neat collection of bags and a bright smile and made marmalade.

When my father finally came home, he spent a long time upstairs in bed and there was a differently strange smell in the bedroom. His left leg was marked with two shiny ovals, bigger than my mother's hand. It looked as if someone had drawn on him with a stencil and then polished his skin like an albino dining table. Each oval was surrounded by ugly black threads with little knots on them. Then these disappeared, leaving a border of pale mauve marks and ridges.

He spent the weekends avoiding the inside of the house. Leaning on the hall windowsill, I could see his corduroy trousers sticking out from under the car, against a background of various greens—the sickly privet and spotted laurel over the road, the bitter green box hedge next door, and the gray-green lamppost rising behind him. The scene, as I looked out, was contained by the neat grid of lead, like a picture in a book of mathematical symmetry. Our garden was filled with his temporary structures. A broken caravan. A homemade tree-house. A lean-to for the mower. Half a green Renault sat on the drive, plundered for parts. I keep this world in the few photographs I have, a dozen round-cornered prints of birthday teas and Christmas trees. I remember it too, in reverse, in the memory of negatives I used to find in boxes. I loved pulling them out of their little pockets in strips, wondering at the inverted world they gave me. The childhood face of my past is pale umber, my pupils translucent, my hair almost black. It is in this looking-glass memory that I get closer to the moment of the taking.

At teatime he came in, washing his hands with green Swarfega before watching the wrestling and the Grand Prix. One of the wrestlers was called Big Daddy, which made me think he might be something to do with God and forgiving our trespasses as we forgive those, but my father told me that his real name was Shirley. Shirley wore an enormous pair of blue-and-white-striped stretch dungarees. He bounced off the ropes and straight into Giant Haystacks. At some point Haystacks bounced up and down on Shirley's stomach and the bell rang. Someone quietly turned the thermostat up.

All houses have their own climate, their own smell, their own temperature and particular ecosystem of air currents and creaks. They all have that specific combination of humid or fetid, of warm or cold that depends on the kind of central heating system you have or do not have, or whether or not the window in the bathroom is open. Smells and sounds can be put into words. Ours had a scent of McVitie's digestive biscuits and furniture polish about it, with a sad hint of hamster in the back living room. A ticking sound as the central heating system turned on and clanged through the pipework. But atmospheres are speechless. When we say that a house has "an atmosphere," it is as if the sentence has given up hope of explaining itself. Atmospheres exist somewhere between sound and silence, and in the pitch and cadences of voices. In a house with an atmosphere, it is as if someone has imperceptibly turned the volume down, and flattened every voice. When there is an atmosphere in a house, a question is answered with silence, or in the way a head is moved just an inch away from center when someone speaks, so that there's space for a roll of the eyes. The television, of course, is the friend of the atmosphere. In periods where the difficulties of shared space and time have felt too much, the television, *eternullity* in a box, gives the bodies within the family permission to stare forward, like communicants at an altar.

My brother once told me that the Germans have a word for that feeling you get on a Sunday afternoon—they call it *Sonntagangst*. I thought he was joking, but held on to the joke nonetheless, as a good way of catching the mood of those suburban weekends. We were stuck in, or under, the grip of it—and I could feel that bored sadness drifting around the room, so strongly I felt that I could almost hold it. Monday sat on the front steps waiting for us, and we thought about its world of beginnings—polishing shoes and washing in the avocado-green plastic bath, with its crack along the front panel. But Sunday afternoons seemed soaked in desolation, as limp as the toast and honey on the blanket-box coffee table. Alain Prost drove his nose around Brands Hatch again and again, the dust flying off the curves of the track, with a sound like someone screaming through the air. Perhaps the most frightening thing about an atmosphere is that it's contagious. It gets everywhere, like glitter. The atmosphere begins when two people refuse to understand each other. She, let us say, wishes to eat a bowl of cornflakes and do some work. He, perhaps, wants to hang out some laundry. She perceives his laundry hanging out to be a tacit criticism of her choice to work. He wonders why she needs four cups to be on the table simultaneously, rather than using the same one each time she makes a cup of tea. Everything about his laundry-collecting is perceived by her to be a kind of aural reproach. The way he is sighing quietly as he untangles a leg of her wet tights that is knotted, lumpily, around the leg of his wet jeans, and the way he hefts the mound of laundry into the basket—both are obviously directed toward her. He sees her gaze into the middle distance, not visibly working, as a sign that she has disconnected, too easily, from the family unit. He walks out of the room carrying the basket. A sock falls out of the silver drum, onto the floor, and she follows him, then feels obliged to join in. They put the smallest wet clothes on children's hangers. He silently corrects the way she carelessly places the socks on the stand, smoothing out the creases that will delay drying time or cause mildew by doubling or tripling the damp factor. Both know they are right. The atmosphere settles in, like mist on an autumn evening. The terrifying thing about it is that atmospheres, like mist, get everywhere. There is no escape. So the two people who are trying to retain autonomy find themselves floating in the same emotional soup. They have seeped into each other. They are both pissed off. Somebody suggests a walk.

I am not a natural walker. I am not a nature person. When people tell me I'm missing out, I know they're probably right, and my mind stamps a petulant and defensive foot. My sympathies lie with another nature unlover. *I don't like mountains*, W. H. Auden's boyfriend told him, when offered a romantic minibreak in the Alps. *I only like towns where there are shops.* Poor Wystan. Poor Gerhart. Sometimes I meanly imagine that everybody else's families dislike the whole walking thing as much as I do. That they're just being dutiful. We should get some air, they say to each other. We ought to stretch our legs. It would be good to get out. I imagine that underneath it all is an unacknowledged desire to escape, if not from each other, then into a kind of fantasy involving Wellington boots, Poohsticks, and a sudden, uncharacteristic interest in wildlife.

Even now, I struggle with the first steps. Standing in the narrow hallway, desperately trying to find coats, hats, missing gloves. Someone complains that their Wellingtons chafe around the lower calf. Someone else cannot do up their zip. Someone scratches their head, and you wonder if they might have nits again. Everybody is finally dressed. Then someone wants a snack, and someone else needs a glass of water. We stand on the flagstones, staring up at the light and the drizzle, and then we all set off. The scenery is different, but the atmosphere persists. Nobody can go too far ahead. You can't give up and dive into a local pub. To walk back home would be to cause a scene. Headphones are generally frowned upon, but you can possibly get away with earmuffs. In some senses, the walk offers family members a good deal *less* freedom. There is no shed to hide in. There are no curtains. You cannot claim exhaustion and take a nap. Everyone must exist in roughly the same geographical arena. Everyone must appear to enjoy the walk (at least moderately). There's a reason one of the greatest novels in English begins with its heroine's delight that there was *no possibility of taking a walk that day*. There are no window seats on family walks. And you can't read a book while walking with your family. There's a reason *Jane Eyre* appeals to teenagers.

Our regular weekend walk in West Finchley was always the same. Out of the front door to the road end where my brother rode his Chopper, and left through the mesh of gates with the notice that read NO HORSE RIDING. Then the muddy path with the tennis courts on our right, the wooden bridge beside the drainage pipe, turning right along the path of the river, and around the corner where the trees thinned out, leaning over the water, the smell of wild garlic overpowering. Then through the winners of the best-kept small lot in Barnet, on the path lined with cow parsley behind netball wire. Sometimes we went across Fursby Avenue to the park with the big swings and the proper silver slide. But that park was far enough away that it never seemed to quite belong to us. Usually we turned around at the final gate and walked back down the river bend, kicking our way through the flattened chestnut branches.

When I was eight, I moved schools, and my father started to take me there on the Tube. The connection from West Finchley was a slow one, as the line divided just before it, at Mill Hill East—so you had to wait that bit longer for the train. The station was in the opposite direction to the woods, off the main road, hidden down a slope, after the Chinese takeout and the post office and Dick's the Grocers, and what was then a chemist but would soon become a video rental store. When my father went into Lovesay & Son to get his paper, I would look up at the pale blue lettering, wondering at the name. Lovesay. Inside, I would stand at the shelves, looking at the rows of sweets. Opal Fruits and Frazzles and Parma Violets became muddled in my mind with the idea of amorous declarations and headlines. A collection of objects hung on the opposite wall, suspended in air like my old Ladybird Key Words book. Watering can. Trowel. Funnel. Bucket.

Mr. Lovesay didn't seem to have a son. He wore a brown shop coat and walked back and forth between the rear of the shop and the counter. Whenever he sold something, he would tear off a small-numbered ticket from a perforated pad. I wondered if love was something you could tear, as well as something you could say.

Every morning, I would have my small travel pass ready to show at the gate where nobody ever stood. We would walk over the latticed bridge and wait for the train, at the far end, past the wooden waiting room, looking up at the sign for NEXT TRAIN. The 1959 stock shuffled out of an invisible siding, confirming itself as via Bank or via Charing Cross, terminating at Morden. This was a world of strange words. *Via. No smoking.* The sliding doors would open and I would take a seat in the nearly empty carriage, feeling the prickly blue-green tartan moquette on the back of my bare legs, and looking at the lined wood floor.

The sign for Lovesay & Son is still there, its pale blue fading into white, like the veins on a porcelain wrist. Dick's the Grocers has long gone, turned into a salon that announces its treatments in a list to the right of the door: *Manicure & Pedicure, Cavitation Weight Loss, Gel & Acrylic Nails, Teeth Whitening, Eyebrow Shaping, Hair Extensions, IPL Hair Removal, Skin Rejuvenation, Microdermabrasion, Botox and Fillers, Massage, Facial, Waxing.* And the Northern Line still has the same two branches going south into London that never meet. We wanted to get onto the other branch, so we always had to go too far to get to where we needed to, and go back out of town again. The first stop of the journey took just moments, a slowish grind past some shrubbery and an arched bridge, but then the train stopped again for ages at Finchley Central, a junction station that looked like a Swiss lodge, all frilled wooden panels and bottle-green paintwork. Finally we sped up on our way to East Finchley (birthplace of Jerry Springer), with its deco staircases in glazed glass tubes. Then we were flying again, past endless allotments, and the rainbow colors of electric cables and the blind backs of houses with their sheds at the bottom of the garden, through a small tunnel, and the Tube really became the Tube, with that familiar *rick-rack* sound, plummeting down under Highgate Hill toward Archway, Tufnell Park, and Kentish Town.

The carriage got crowded around about Highgate, and then my father stood above me in his suit, holding on to one of the fiberglass globes on bendy springs, swaying until the crush of bodies in the carriage held him still. He was one of many commuters crammed into this train in the spring of 1983. They all looked the same—the million Mr. Averages switching on for work. George Michael wore blue jeans rolled up at the ankle and white trainers and a black leather jacket. They wore navy mackintoshes and pinstriped suits. Looking up at the sea of gray Denby-pressed fabric, I reached out to steady myself on the wrong legs.

Camden was a crush of bodies moving this way and that through the various tunnels, taking the "via Bank" people onward to Charing Cross, allowing those who were journeying on the two branches of the northern bit of the Northern Line to swap over. But the platform to Edgware and Colindale was always quieter and the train was nearly empty. By 8 a.m. we were heading back out to the suburbs up the other branch, making what on the map looked like exactly the same journey, but backward, and five centimeters lower down.

There were no escalators at Belsize Park. The lifts were closed with expanding iron doors, like a concertina cage, and they juddered their way up to the surface. Once the lift broke and we made our way up the steps, circling into the same gray rain and red brick of Haverstock Hill—the place where the not-suburban people lived.

Much of that journey is now, for me, not lost, but trapped in time. Just one of the ways that time tends to trap us. Everything about that journey was regularized too. There is something about the world of commuting that washes a sense of difference out of things and people. Commuters may look the same. Every day, they inhabit the same space. They follow the same timetable. They ride the same train. People, like trains, were regular beings. They did not transform, or mutate. They did not go changing.

Wishing for difference was one of my favorite childhood activities. On the way to school each day, I read on the train. I'd like to think my father did too. But the books lined up on the bookshelf at home—*The Day of the Triffids, Rumpole, The Great Railway Bazaar, Homage to Catalonia*—didn't look like the sort of things you'd carry on the Tube in the morning. If I strain my memory hard, perhaps he is holding a newspaper, or a last-minute sheaf of figures. As I sat there on my itchy seat, I read in envy of other people's hair and clothes, their houses and their relatives, their food and their wallpaper. I read because other people's halls were invariably bigger than ours. Other people's houses had multiple floors. Other people's mothers wore sunglasses. Other people's families took me out for lunch to restaurants that served puddings called *The Outrageous*. Other people's fathers carried mobile phones.

Even when they were doing nothing, other people's families did it better than mine. On a Saturday afternoon, the

Bakers stretched out on a chaise longue or lay on the floor reading newspapers. The Shermans faced each other across the shag pile in articulated padded loungers, drinking frozen orange juice from individual snack trays. The Greens had a swimming pool and a petting zoo. Life was an Argos catalogue of alternative possibilities, and envy was my hobby and my salvation. I was an expert in it.

Going through East Finchley, I read on—for other, better homes and better stories. *Ballet Shoes* on the Brompton Road. Windsor Gardens. Avonlea. Tara. Kansas. Oz. I read of *The Ordinary Princess* and Minnie the Minx. I read of Peter and Mollie and the Wishing-Chair with its bulbous legs and temperamental little red wings. I loved the shiny blue hardback cover, Mollie's hairband and ponytail combo, and the spiked violet creams that did for the Ho-ho Wizard. Most of all, I loved the scene where Mollie and Peter's mother takes a liking to their flying chair and brings it into the house. Then Mollie, pretty Mollie, who never does anything out of turn, goes for the Enid Blyton equivalent of juvenile delinquency. She thinks up the *deliberately naughty* idea of vandalizing it in order to get it back, taking the sewing scissors to the cushion, spilling ink on the upholstery, and kicking the legs until it is ruined.

I wanted to vandalize their chair too—not to help them, but because I wanted what they had and I couldn't. Peter and Mollie had an Emergency Exit. If I were them, I could fly out of the window, out of the semi-detached world. I read on. Addicted to the kind of novels in which exceptionally ordinary children are "discovered" by directors and thrust upon the stage, I stared at the man who got on the train at Kentish Town, who could have been a casting agent. If I stared hard enough, perhaps my story would transform itself into something else, something extraordinary.

There is something childlike in memory, which makes me conceive of my father as a perpetual commuter. Though the act of remembering him is sudden (it lands with violence, like a carriage lurching off the rails), the image of him is steady in my mind. And the picture that unfolds is predictable, regular, moving according to a pattern I have long established.

We are walking out of the station. He holds my schoolbag in one hand and encloses my hand in the other. His are large and blunt-fingered, with freckled backs, rough from fixing cars, but soft to touch. Over five days, he explains to me exactly how a carburetor works. I listen, with half an ear, trying to understand, but also just following the rise and fall of his voice.

When he dropped me at the gates, he handed over my satchel, and turned to smile and wave. He was an enigma to me, as he floated off to an office in a place called Elephant and Castle. I imagined it as a place of Eastern mystery, with turreted castles and elephants floating on clouds, dozens of them in diagonal lines, like wallpaper, ridden by men in suits. After he said goodbye, I looked for a moment at his long gray-legged figure walking down the road, holding the image, and then turned away. Standing there, I never thought about where he would be going next. It didn't occur to me that to get me there he was going round in circles, heading back once more down the same line—turning again in order to go on.

# BAKER STREET TO MOORGATE STREET

NINE YEARS AFTER THAT GOODBYE IN NEW YORK, KATE Field came to London and set up a temporary home there for the next few winters. She would have needed that umbrella. The weather was predictably terrible, a *pasticcio of rain*, she called it, and endless fog. For two days, an enormous fall of snow brought everything to a halt. The brougham cabs refused to leave their stands, with an enterprising few hiking their fares at night to a surge rate. Field took to walking everywhere, her skirts shortened to save them from the gray slush on the pavement. The flash of black gumboot underneath mystified the boot blacks sitting on the street corners. She rode the omnibus to Baker Street, where she walked past the Smithfield poultry show, to stare at a wax model of the Nawab Gholam Hussein Khan, resplendent in his green and gold, standing next to the latest version of the Prince of Wales. She visited the Zoological Gardens and spoke at public dinners, went from St. George-in-the-East to Belgravia, and from Jamroab's Wild Beast Bazaar to Parliament itself. She sat on the earliest version of the Circle Line, yet to become a circle, making her way from Baker Street to Moorgate Street, up the Metropolitan Line.

In those days, the Underground was crawling around London like a giant caterpillar, chewing up the pavements and creating enormous piles of earth. As new stations were built, people picked their way on planks toward their houses. You can see photographs of its making—three workmen staring at the camera with their arms crossed, a rare recorded sighting of Britain's black Victorians. Soon, the idea of traveling in a tunnel became a fact of life. People were becoming accustomed to the sight of carriages appearing from archways, into the grubby twilight, with the silhouette of St. Paul's in the background. Used to the turnstiles and tickets and the confusion of losing things in the hurry.

Today, the Circle Line still isn't a real circle—invaded at all angles by the District and Metropolitan, kinked at Edgware Road. One wrong move at Earl's Court and it can still send you round in an unwitting loop, circling back to where you began. Nowadays, the trains are sleek silver beasts, joined with gray rubber concertinas, which bend and flex with the tessellated sheets of metal as if they are alive, breathing with the train's movement, like a big anemone. But some things are the same. At Sloane Square, a man in a red beanie hat will play the tune from *The South Bank Show* on his violin, then hold out a paper cup for donations—the look in his eyes not perhaps that different from those of the many hungry men, women, and children who have made their way across the pavements of Praed Street over the years, players in the station game. The District and Circle commuter sways to the rhythm of the metal heartbeat, wearing his suit and anorak, just as his great-great-grandfather would have stood, carried through the same tunnels, twenty-five feet of cut and cover under the surface of London.

It is cleaner now, of course. Dirt was everywhere when Kate Field rode the Underground. The air was full of the sound of carriage doors slamming shut, drafts of air coming down the tunnels, and the acrid smoke that caught in the back of your throat and made you cough. The swaying gas-lit orbs would have given everything a smoky, ochre tone. George Gissing wrote of the black fumes, the shrill whistles, the walls of adverts that clamored to the eye: theaters, journals, soaps, medicines, concerts, furniture, wines, prayer meetings. Field would have looked out over the sea of workmen's caps and tall top hats and thin umbrellas and greenish newspapers folded in a hurry. She would have covered her mouth and made for the Moorgate Street exit.

London had made Field sick before. She was laid low one winter for three weeks with bronchitis, but this time she was better insulated, taking rooms in New Cavendish Street on the corner near Wimpole Street, which she decorated with newspapers and photographs. She needed her voice more than ever. She was in charge of promoting the eighth wonder of the world as the first public relations manager for Alexander Graham Bell's new invention, the telephone.

Field believed in the telephone. Love at first sight. She writes of the excitement of approaching the small pear-shaped wooden instrument, which sat on a desk, looking for all the world like a misplaced stethoscope. And then her surprise when she picked it up—hearing a voice. A speaking object. Intimacy at a distance. Soon, she said, *every house will be connected*. Everyone wanted to see this invention, and Field was its natural promoter. She conjured an air of mystique around the new, otherworldly piece of technology. Invitations were issued to select VIP salon events, or telephone séances. This was the age of spiritualism, an age of table rapping and mesmerism, and the papers loved it. There were special guests, and celebrity visits. Prince Louis Napoleon turned up with the Duchess of Westminster and a large party of swells. George Eliot got her own private audience with the device, and a special telephone concert was fixed for Queen Victoria. Always ahead of her time, Field pitched a Zoom prototype as the next step.

All through the winter and spring of 1878, invited guests gathered in the Cannon Street offices. Bell took center stage, placing the sacred instrument on a wooden platform. MPs and aristocrats chatted, lunched, and talked politics, while they viewed and heard their voices make their way down the wires. The whole thing must have taken the edge off the melancholy weather and rising tensions in Constantinople. Field took notes, made introductions, hustled. Hidden in the guest list, somewhere between the actress Lillie Langtry and the publisher John Blackwood, was her friend Anthony Trollope.

When I was growing up, every phone call was a small journey. I would emerge from my bedroom at the back of the house, along the landing and past the airing cupboard, running my hand along the Anaglypta wallpaper, round and down the stairs to the front hall, where the beige plastic phone sat on the window ledge, beside the address book and a pot of pens. Looking out of the window, you'd see the silver birch, then Mavis Pace's house opposite, with the white, glass-paneled front door lined with net that felt like silk.

Our phone had a transparent dial—a circle, divided in half, with a piece of paper in the center bearing the number and code, and made of two bits of plastic, with a grooved line in between to collect grit. Even the act of using the phone was a journey in miniature. Every one of the seven digits involved the slow pulling back, and releasing, of the rotary dial. If your courage faltered, you could stop at any moment, and fiddle with the grit in the telephone case, or try to clear the white mist from the leadlighting with your thumbnail, until the final number was pulled back and the recoil spring took matters into its own hands. Then your only choice was to listen to the sound of ringing, or slam the receiver down before the other person answered.

Field and Trollope sat together in that sunny room in Cannon Street surrounded by the throng of guests. Was there something between them—a hint of smoke in the air? Perhaps they'd arrived together. Perhaps Trollope had written her one of his notes—*If you like it I will take you. I will call for you at 3 p.m. in a hansom cab. Let me have a line to say so.* Trollope was always waiting on a line from Field. We have the record of his invitations. His letters. Their implications. *If you'll go down close to the sea, & near enough for me to get at you, I would then go to you.* He sends her a kiss that is as loving as you please. In another, he talks of something darker—the black phantom that lies between them, that vexes her, and teases his wife. In one short story he tells of a sleigh ride with a woman who sounds uncannily like Field. They sit, side by side, all enveloped in buffalo furs, and he thinks how nice it would be to drive on and on, so that nobody should ever catch them. He felt he would have liked to cross the Rocky Mountains with her, over to the Pacific, and to have come home round by California, Peru, and the Pampas. Everywhere, moving.

Trollope asks her again, in a letter, to meet. He writes of her with love. She is a ray of light to him. She is someone from whom he can always strike a spark. He asks for her to come and see him. Field's replies are lost.

Perhaps there's a pile of letters and telegrams somewhere. But that month, at least, I suspect she simply had little time for correspondence. Maybe she barely even noticed Trollope was there at all. Or perhaps she invited him just so that he could watch her show off, flirting with John Everett Millais or giving Lady Henniker the eye. It could have been a kind of revenge. The first time they had met, in Italy, when all eyes were on him, Field had sat in the corner feeling like a nobody, waiting to catch his attention. Now she was in the center, holding court, one of the "taking" things of the season. Either way, there would have been a moment when she passed the receiver to him. He could have still felt the warmth of her hand on the wood.

How long can two people be apart from one another—how many impossibilities between them—before the connection goes dead?

The journey to an affair is like the longest dialing process in the world. Most of the time we never go further than rifling through our mental address book, looking at names and checking their Twitter feed, wondering what they might be up to. Thinking about who and what might happen if you ever called, and if they would choose to pick up. Perhaps they are already on another line.

But sometimes you press the final number, the fatal digit, and you hear it ring. You proceed to pass Go. You plan and choose what to wear, and buy a ticket, and get on the train, with an excuse in your pocket. You watch the people reading their books—facing each other, back-to-back. Then you step off the Overground and walk down to the slip road as night falls—and there are still a hundred moments when you can turn back. You can stop at the wharf and think it through, remembering how to compose your life in a way that won't hurt you, or others. You can stand near the boats and the old warehouses and look at the way the metalwork frames the canal, before walking back down the road to the station. But you don't. You keep walking and cross the road, turn right after the bridge, following the bend of the path with the stretch of graffiti. The buildings close in on you as you enter the yard. There's a tension as you get nearer the door. A moment of space that feels as if you're falling into a doubly indrawn breath—then you press the bell. You know you really should be somewhere else. And up until that moment you can always turn back, or turn aside.

Then you have done it, and the door clicks open. The recoil spring takes over. Before that moment, though, you are waiting, turning, watching the wheel spin.

You are free, even if pulled by an ache lodged somewhere between your shoulder and your heart. All my life I've made journeys like this, detours from the track that I'm meant to be on. The journey feels like a way to a cure, even as it speaks of an illness. Some of us have loved this journey itself most of all, loved it more than arriving.

# MOSCOW

ANNA DESCENDS FROM THE NIGHT TRAIN INTO THE EARLY morning gray, stepping down from the steep carriage stairs and onto the platform of bags and porters and cabs waiting to pick up fares. She would have reached the station at 11 a.m. Moscow time. (That said, all time was Moscow time on Russian trains, which meant that if you were on a train near Ekaterinburg wanting blini for breakfast, you could end up being offered cabbage soup for lunch.)

Like all good travelers, she kept her luggage near her. Standing there, on the platform, in her dark traveling coat and hat, watching the movement at the station, the entrances and exits. She would have had a trunk or two—and a valise. Perhaps a shawl or rug over an arm. And a red silk pouch, her мешочек, would have hung from her wrist—just large enough to carry her most immediate possessions. Tolstoy's wife, Sofia, had three or four bags like this—some beaded, some fabric, some finished with braid, formed in each corner with two loops.

Once you start looking through the novel, bags are all over the place. A rash of them. They break out like measles, all crimson and leather, in chapter after chapter. After her first disturbing and thrilling encounter with the handsome officer, Vronsky, Anna hides her face from her sister-in-law's gaze. She bends her flushed face over a tiny bag, stowing her nightcap and handkerchiefs. Later this is the bag where she keeps her books, the tiny pocket editions of English novels that provide their own ways and places to hide. Anna's handbag is an opening to a world of her own, her way of knowing that she might walk free and away in a blaze of red. But it's also a sign of retreat. Holding her nightcap and handkerchiefs, her modesty, it keeps Anna steady. There is, for her, no other gathering point.

So everyday in their existence, we barely register how bags are entwined with the world of secrets and power, money and myth. They are not kept close to our body, like a pocket, nor do they live apart from us, like a safe, or a chest. Prosthetic extensions. Intimate, but at arm's length. The bag is a way of managing space. We condense our lives into stuff, squeeze it into pockets and compartments, shut clasps and buckles and zips—so we can take some of our space with us as we travel. And, unless you're a fan of transparent handbags (big in the 1960s), they also provide a private space in the public world. Even within our houses, a bag usually belongs to one individual. We rarely share them. They are our bastion, our fortress, our protection from communal space. They are the first place we hide things and the first place you would look to find something hidden. A Hermès Birkin sold in 2018 at Christie's auction house for the price of a very small flat on the outermost reaches of London. White crocodile skin, encrusted with 10.23 carats of diamonds. There's a museum entirely devoted to the history of handbags in a canal-side house in Amsterdam. There you'll find the early leather sacks carried by men, embroidered and inlaid reticules once held by grand Georgian ladies. The bags are back-lit, hanging from hooks in cabinets—and the whole thing feels like an incredibly high-end charity shop. Many of the bags have some kind of story about them. A French beaded pouch commemorates the arrival of Zarafa the Nubian giraffe in Paris's Jardin des Plantes. A clutch bag is made in the shape of an ocean liner. Others are more personal celebrations—miniatures of two newlyweds are embedded into the front flap of a delicate peach silk bag. Some are transparent, shaped like Cinderella's carriage. A sequin-encrusted can of Coke, a fairy cake on a strap. Famous bags sit with everyday bags. Madonna's bag outshines the one that belonged to Imelda Marcos. There's something that looks like a nineteenth-century changing bag, with a deco-rative feature of a mother and a child in a playpen. There's a 1920s Egyptian-style bag decorated with lapis lazuli. In the tearoom, admiring postcards of bags and bag paraphernalia, surrounded by paintings of Roman gods and goddesses, you can wonder at the felicitous coincidence that Charles-Émile Hermès, the Parisian leatherworker whose company went on to create some of the world's most iconic bags, shared his name with the nearest we have to the god of luggage. Hermes—god of boundaries and doorways, the traveling god, god of trade and commodities, always depicted with a satchel on his arm.

A latter-day Anna Karenina would, I imagine, go bag shopping in the big department store on Nevsky Prospekt, with its arcades and concessions, its peculiar holiday lights and stiff, half-dressed mannequins. There the bags sit side by side, looking pristine and oddly ridiculous. What is a bag without an owner? She would dismiss the cheaper brands, not even glancing at the rucksacks on the ground floor. The special cases of little Picard and Moschino bags look nearer to what a twenty-first-century Anna might carry, but it's still hard to pin it down. Bags, after all, are a personal thing.

Maybe our Anna would have gone bespoke—had one made in the latest style by one of the haberdashers in St.

Petersburg. Her sister-in-law, Dolly, would not have thought to carry a *sac à main* or reticule. She probably disapproved. The conservative papers called them *ridicules*. Anna's bag was a public sign that she could be a woman and a mobile agent. She could walk alone—and make her own choices— in public. A bag of one's own meant a purse of one's own. It meant she had the power to spend. Her handbag came into fashion at the same moment as the arrival of the department store—and was a portable license to enter a utopia. The larger bags had room for everything—the *cartes de visite*, the ivory notepad and address book, the candy box and the mirror, the rice-powder puff, the tiny handkerchief, the rouge. But bags were manacles as much as miracles. They made the execution more and more difficult. Those, like Anna, who carried them were making a kind of declaration. Both showing and hiding all the stuff a woman needed to keep the fiction going.

I remember tagging along with my brother on my mother's biennial handbag-shopping expeditions. We would always go to the enormous shopping center, north London's flag-ship attempt at the American mall, built on the site of a sewage works and a greyhound stadium. There we would stand in the concrete marvel, staring at the people who had enough money to eat in the sunken café surrounded by silver railings. We were allowed to stand for five minutes by the enormous fountain beside Lilley and Skinner, watching the shoppers ride the escalator over it, as if entering another world. I remember listening to its roar and feeling the cool air—a kind of postmodern Niagara Falls. At the counter, in the leather, jewelry, and gifts section, my mother would range for what felt like hours, comparing two seemingly identical models of navy-blue Tula bags, checking that the number of compartments and zips was suitable for use, would prevent pilfering, would allow for diary fitting, and ensure comfort. I could sense that this purchase was not a pleasure for her. It seemed freighted with all the things she had to bear. This life was not her bag, as it were. Sitting under the clothes rail, I came to a realization that being a grown-up meant spending a lot of money on a sensible navy-blue bag that would go over one's shoulder. I vowed I would never carry one.

Fashion bloggers make choosing a handbag sound like a v. big deal. The ideal handbag is not just a microcosm of our world and identity but also a bit like choosing a life partner. There's a real language of commitment about it. A new hand-bag will be a constant companion that will migrate easily from one situation to another. Some bags may be celebrations, representing a key moment in an individual's handbag journey. Only one can emerge as the Holy Grail Bag, the one that must complement all our changing moods, yet still be consistent to our inner self.

As if.

I have been untrue to my inner self. Today I own a moderate collection of relatively nasty and sensible bags. In my wardrobe, there's a blue leather one with a fabric lining that I thought might make me look sort of upbeat and perky but which I've managed to look frumpy in. I've a navy mock-croc number that I got cheap on eBay. I thought I might manage to look chic and grown-up with it, but whenever I pick it up I feel like Margaret Thatcher. I've got an enormous leather sack with a broken lining. It looks quite nice, but everything I own slides down between the leather and the lining, causing frenetic scrabbling in train stations for purse and keys. And then there's the sensible brown one I'm using at the moment. It looked OK online, but in reality it is so obviously fake leather, and the zips and straps jangle in a way that seems designed to irritate the wearer. I also have a satchel with a broken strap, and a selection of rucksacks (orange, gray, and gold), which I bought in a fit of hatred of ladylike handbags. I dislike and resent all bags, in different and complicated ways. They all seem like a public declaration. A statement that I must keep things about myself conventionally hidden from view, safely stowed away. My favorite bag in the Dutch museum is the one that looks like an alarm clock—round, hanging from a chain, its dial face directed outward as it bangs against the hip. Because bags also tell us something about our place in time as well as in space. They hold our past and our future. They carry our money, our receipts, our tissues, and our tampons. They speak of contingency and autonomy. They store the things we can't quite bring ourselves to leave behind, or have forgotten that we don't need anymore. A pair of broken sunglasses, the residue of a broken heart, a magazine, a button, a paperclip in the shape of a spiral.

An American hiker has become famous for walking the roads with a bag no larger than a child's knapsack. He leaves possessions behind. He is freeing himself of anxiety, he says. Each object in a bag represents a particular fear: of injury, of discomfort, of boredom, of attack. (This sounds good on paper, but it's probably easier to live in the present if you don't bleed every month.) The hiker's future fears are hypothetical. For some of us, they are not so much fears as inevitable happenings. But something of this still makes sense to me. A bag is a container of emotion. The ever-steady Mary Poppins—the ideal mother-substitute, always there but never feeling. Hers is an impossible vortex of a bag. A magical carpetbag with no floor. It contains everything from a potted palm to a standard lamp. Perhaps even her tears.

As I sit here now, I am less held than I am a holding bay. A place for hopes and hands, attention and tissues. My handbag's contents are partially mine, but also my children's—I carry their treasures, their games, and their rubbish in equal measure. Along with my copy of *Anna Karenina*, it contains, in no particular order: a Shrinky Dink pirate picture (half colored-in), a container of Lightning McQueen bubble mixture (nearly empty), a pair of socks, an old ham sandwich (still in foil), a tube of roll-on sun cream (sensitive), a pack of Top Trumps cards (Avengers), a Smashbox lipstick (First Time), one chocolate croissant (stale, still in its bag), one piece of toast (in a napkin), seven bus tickets, a hairbrush (with hair).

It's embarrassing. It weighs me down. Not just the bag, but the unwritten law that suggests I should conceal my apparatus from view. The rules of privacy are an imposition. I fantasize about walking over a motorway bridge, opening my bag, and watching its contents fall onto the passing cars, pencil sharpenings and sticky pennies and all. Even having the time to wonder about this is a sign of my secure world, my excessive consumption, my middle-class privilege, my luck. But there's something more. Something in this that irritates me enough to press on it. Just within my grasp, like an object that has disappeared into a tear in the lining and can only be felt. However petty it may seem to want a bag of my own—or no bag—when my bag is so full of plenty, I do not want to give up on my small rage just yet. It touches on something more than half the world knows, in one form or another.

I think of my husband. A phone. A wallet. He has pockets.

Bag ladies—where the public and private collide. Our insides are guessed at from the outside. Surmised. There's the assumption that you should want to be full of someone else. All those questions.

Are you trying?

Don't leave it too late.

You should get breeding. (Don't want to be an old bag.) And the implications, the insinuations. Once you have carried another person, you are reshaped, remolded by others. And often not in a good way. Any vision of my pregnant self as a cauldron of life, burgeoning wolf-woman, soon evaporated. In public, I became the human equivalent of one of those nylon money belts—safe, practical, but best left at home on a night out. I have lost myself.

Anna gets this. She has two children—and wants to have no more. She explains to her disbelieving sister-in-law that despite having a lover, she knows for sure that she will never become pregnant again.

Between the lines, Tolstoy hints at one important item in Anna's handbag—an early form of the diaphragm, a womb veil. Anna's handbag has a double life. It is, perhaps, both surrogate womb and a protest against having a womb at all.

Those bags haunt the novel. Again and again, through Tolstoy's words, we will watch her opening and closing its clasps, packing it with items and pulling others out, hiding her face in it as she rearranges its contents. The bag itself seems to have a life of its own, changing shape as the chapters unfurl. Midway through the book, it is described as large enough to hold a small cushion. Sometimes it seems more like an evening bag. As Anna's selfhood diminishes, so perhaps does her luggage. Or maybe Anna has many bags—some large, some small, but most of them red. Maybe Tolstoy doesn't want to be weighed down by the details of luggage. He didn't need to, I suppose.

But Anna's smallest bag—the little red one (her мешочек)—really matters. It is her shield and her burden. Her way of surviving. The little red bag seems to be the one space that Anna can call her own. It is her companion on her travels—a small thing that stands for so much more.

# HACKNEY WICK
## —2006—

HOURS WOULD PASS WITHOUT US TALKING. YOU WORKED IN your studio. I sat on the window seat, my boots and back braced against the alcove. I was paid by the word to write about other people's words. Honing a line. Finding a place to stand in relation to others.

One day, while fiddling with a lamp, you ask why I don't write something people might actually want to read. Get to read.

I watch as you adjust the light meter.

It takes a while for a subject to come into focus.

After rush hour, I pack my possessions up carefully and head back on the stopping service to my two small rooms. I left nothing behind, apart from that mark on the window-seat wall, which I've never told you about.

# GOOLE TO
# THORNE NORTH
## —2016—

CRANES AND COOLING TOWERS ARE HAZY IN THE DISTANCE. Kylie Minogue sits by the edge of a swimming pool, enormous and blonde in her eyewear. The poster girl of solitude. People leave the train, duly reminded to make sure they have taken all their personal possessions with them.

Someone will no doubt have left something behind. Someone always does. Human nature to scatter ourselves carelessly around—a subconscious desire, perhaps, to leave a trace, a fragment of what we once were, abandoned in transit as we go on our way.

There are different textures of loss. The lost we hope to find again, and the lost that we think is gone forever. The loss of an object in the silt of mud, the loss of a smell or a sound. People are lost to us, or make themselves irretrievable. They seek loss. A hundred years before my birth, among the classified sections of *The Times*, there are all of these things— page after page of absence. A catalogue of despondencies, absent-mindedness, ache.

A carriage clock is left in a cab from St. Pancras to Westminster on Monday last. A lady's sealskin muff-bag, containing articles of jewelry, is lost in a first-class carriage of a local train on the Great Northern Railway, on a Monday afternoon. There are things people seemed to lose a lot in those days. Keys, bond shares, purses and small bags (generally containing money, as well as, sometimes, nothing of value except papers, which are important only to the owner). They lose their watches, their rings and their lockets, their bracelets and other jewelry. Dogs, opera glasses and pencil cases, Bank of England notes and spectacles are misplaced or abandoned or stolen. Each loss feels like a novel in miniature. A roll call of lost objects in 1875 brings some poetic specifics: a London dock warrant, a cane of Brazilian palm, a map of the British Channel, an opal brooch, a small case of surgical instruments. On August 12, an aeronautical pioneer seems strangely deflated.

> BALLOON LOST. Started from Taunton at 3 o'clock. Direction about a line from Taunton to Chepstow— Joseph Simmons, Aeronaut, 38, Regent-street, London, W.

There are the sadnesses of letters, possibly lost. Someone who calls themselves AMULET complains of not hearing from their correspondent on Tuesday. Perhaps it was never sent. There are some strangely coded missives. I look at one placed on Christmas Eve, 1875:

> WILL a Black Swan glide again to the entrance of a stream? Exit on last occasion more hurried than graceful. Same address.—GRAPE AND SEALSKIN.

I long to know who GRAPE AND SEALSKIN was or were. Did the Black Swan ever arrive? It seems a language buried too deep to recover, lost in time.

People are missing too. A young gentleman, age 26, height 5 feet 6 inches, fair and pale complexion, was last seen at Charing Cross. It's often young men who disappear (some presumed to have enlisted). But women young and old vanish too—some, in Hitchcockian fashion, have vanished on trains before arriving at their appointed destination. One gentleman with very depressed and emaciated appearance: walks with short steps, and narrow feet not turned out, disappeared while looking much troubled in mind. I worry for those left behind. The costly ads.

Every day of the year seems to bring new trauma, large and small. On January 4, along with a lost gold Albert chain, there is an advert placed for Fred D.L., its tone hovering somewhere between the plaintive and the demanding.

> If you have any regard for yourself and your family, WRITE, or telegraph at once to B.S., and say when and where you will meet him.

January brings further losses, in trains and cabs and hearts. A black bearskin carriage rug, lined in red, is left in a brougham; a brown leather case, well labeled, on a first-class carriage from Ealing. Fred D.L.'s family continue to ask for him. There is a letter for him at the General Post Office. He must not fail to call for it. Someone called A.T. has left. If they return at once, all will be forgiven. T. writes to W. for £20. They are still very ill. The doctor says there is no cure.

A lady's black silk umbrella, ebony handle, with a carved pug on the top ring, has gone astray in the last fortnight, along with a black leather porte-monnaie purse containing a first-class return ticket to Barnet. A son admonishes his mother. He has nothing to say. Someone has received a black bag from Newton. They are full of love and pity and entreat a reader to write. No inquiries will be made.

Two manuscripts are lost. One has been borrowed and not returned. The other left in a hansom cab in Fleet Street, wrapped in a sheet of *The Times*. People hesitate about where exactly something was lost. Either in Chapel-street or Belgrave-square. Between Kew-bridge and the Strand, via South-Western Railway and Waterloo-Bridge, near Paddington Terminus. It is hard to retrace your steps when they have wandered.

A black portmanteau has been taken by mistake. The owner of the similar one, unclaimed at Victoria Station, will have been surprised to find a case full of baby's linen.

Heart-shaped gold lockets are lost. Presumably hearts too. E.P., who left Eastbourne by the 2 p.m. train for Victoria on Monday, and was expected at a station on the Sevenoaks line, is earnestly requested to communicate with one of his anxious relatives. Perhaps he wants to be lost. Many do. Maybe the thirty-year-old woman with dark brown hair, dark blue eyes, and a slight limp, who left Sheffield for her home in Devon, but disappeared at Paddington Station, wanted not to be found. Four children, aged nine, seven, five, and two, disappeared with her.

So many of these missing people seem like ghosts:

MYSTERIOUSLY DISAPPEARED from her home, on Friday, the 5th inst., a YOUNG MARRIED LADY, 24 years of age, tall and upright, straight dark hair, dark eyes, finely arched eyebrows, very pale complexion; lisps slightly when speaking; was dressed in gray silk dress (two shades), moleskin jacket, black bonnet, with white feather. INFORMATION of her present whereabouts will be most handsomely REWARDED.

So fine and slight and pale. She is destined to vanish, to dwindle away. I wish her luck. A shade (two shades) in Victorian limbo.

There are many lost letters, and lost addresses. Quite a few lost tempers. Writes THE ONE OF THE VALLEY—*You do not know how sorry you have made me. Farewell*. There are ongoing stories, too, some of which stretch across the years: Mrs. T is concerned about the well-being and whereabouts of Mrs. M. Jones for at least two years in the 1870s; W. writes that he wishes to see his friend at ninety-six, particularly at regular intervals throughout the same time period. Others are brighter, shorter-lived flames. What trouble was Fred D.L. in, I wonder? Did he ever get out of it? I see the reaching out of nearly lost hopes. *Write to me*, one advertiser begs. *Do not fear about the thing lost.*

*Have you forgotten me and the pretty gardens?* asks M. *Will you write, or call?*

Or a simple message to Henry—*Your return will be most welcome.*

No doubt whole conversations, indeed whole lives, are hidden here in these classified columns. An exhibition of loss. Take the one from February 9, 1875:

BR.—Same address. Nothing constant. Wants.

# HACKNEY WICK
## —2006—

OUR FIGHTS ALWAYS BEGAN AS I WAS LEAVING FOR THE STA-tion. Always after it had been a lovely day, a lovely weekend. A wonderland of photographs and sex. Meeting your beautiful friends in beautiful houses. Pretending that's all we were. Meet my assistant, you said to them. They looked at me with a raised eyebrow. We went to someone's fiftieth birthday party. I made my way around the groups, losing sight of you in the paths around the middle, but always hearing your voice over the others, seeing you out of the corner of my eye. We would stop, late and hungry, at a restaurant, and collapse into bed. You promised we would talk about what we were, where we were. You always said that we would talk about our destination. Tomorrow.

We often went nowhere. Or just out on the Tube and back.

If anyone had looked down on us, I think we would have looked like shop mannequins of sorts, plasticized and stiff, adopting the posture of a couple that we had never learned to be.

The next morning we would wake up late and screw and fall asleep, and the time had gone. Lust or love flickered around us, somewhere in the movement of estrogen or testosterone, dopamine or norepinephrine. A drop in serotonin, a surge of oxytocin.

I had to go to work, for my half job. No time for conversation now as I began to pack my bag. Leaning on the door jamb, you told me that you loved me. What more did I want. This was your life. I was part of it. Could we just *not worry* about the future. Already as you spoke I could see you in your mind, getting behind your lens, disappearing as if down a circle of glass. You were beginning to see the light. To make a good picture. I attempted to master the trick of closing the zip of my bag over the lumps created by my trainers. It nearly closed, leaving a small opening at one end. The fabric was pulled painfully tight. I made my way down in the lift, on my own. Somewhere near Highbury, it started to come undone.

# THORNE NORTH
# TO DONCASTER

## —2016—

TWO MEN ON THE PLATFORM IN SAFETY JACKETS ARE crouching over a station lamppost, which has collapsed onto itself like an overgrown tulip. The woman across my aisle has finished refolding her kite and is now coloring in a picture of a squirrel. The other woman has put away her half-eaten Kinder Bueno in the plastic bag at her feet.

There were a few moments of silence before I left home. It will be silent again as I come back through the door. When I turn off the lights and walk up to bed, I will tread on something, because I always do. Perhaps a sneaker, or a piece of toast, or a discarded plastic penguin. Tomorrow will be busy with small acts of tidying up. I wish I didn't have to. When I get to be alone, I make a mess. I put teacups and cereal bowls in the bathroom sink. I eat out of a frying pan, sitting on the kitchen floor. I drop clothes on the stairs and leave a ring of shaved leg hair round the bath. I go to the loo and sit there and type. I get an intense kind of pleasure from this behavior. As a messy person living with other less messy people, these spells of solitude are an oasis, a few hours when I can release my inner slob.

Twenty years ago, I could do this all the time, albeit in a smaller arena. I lived in one or two rooms, pretty much, and always in a mess. The wardrobe doors were left open, clothes spread out in an unbroken carpet from the wardrobe floor to the bed, a jumbled pile hanging off the chair. Dirty underwear mixed with old receipts and books. An overflowing wastepaper bin sat in the corner and a number of mugs and empty Pot Noodle containers near the bed, which was also my sofa—the same fold-out foam futon I had slept on as a child.

Mess has a meaning. It is a real habitat—and one that I miss. It stands, partly, for privacy and freedom. If we exist in two spheres, the public and the private, then the messy room of my own was more private than most. A house, after all, is always partially invaded. A house may not seem public in the way that a street or a park is, but beyond the world of plastic toys and toasters there is always a family show on the road, a communal commitment. The front sitting room, the front door flanked by wellies, the front garden, the way the shutters in front look from the street. Keeping the display going takes effort.

My small bedsit existence was, for the most part, free of these demands. I liked the mess in itself. I liked what it did even more. It kept people out. It kept me in. When I walked home and someone asked to come in for the night, I would remember the extravagant, jaw-dropping quality of my mess—the open tampon box on the windowsill, the lidless empty tube of hair-removal cream left inexplicably on the desk, the half-eaten plate of food on the floor, the unchanged bedding. Self-disgust and shame would win out over loneliness, and I'd say goodbye on the doorstep. Untidiness was my own advanced kind of barrier method.

A divorce barrister once told me that a third of marriages break down over issues concerning cleaning and chores. I moderate my messiness now, out of sympathy for my husband, who looks at my trails of clutter with dismay. But the urge to make a mess is strong in me. It's still there, trying to take over.

My messiness is a kind of play, too—a light rebellion, a denial of responsibility. I am what some, my husband included, might call a *mess terrorist*, using mess to define my own identity at others' expense. But the mess-theorists (there really are mess-theorists) point out that there can be a surprising creativity in mess. Those who refuse to live in time and space tidily, who live an *improvisational* life, can stumble across revelations as they stub their toe. Sometimes I tidy up. But even then I keep my mess close to me, in small middens in drawers, behind screens, in plastic bags full of junk hanging over the banisters. My discarded mugs of coffee breed under the bed like mushrooms, colonizing, encroaching. My mess is an abortive force, relentless, trying to make itself known. I think of the table back home, with its mess of lunch boxes and computer cables, baby wipes and bills, with a sort of pride.

Messiness is a key part of the art of losing. Mess gives us a world in which to play with loss. To misplace things. In a messy room, or house, stuff can disappear, but not the knowledge that it still exists, somewhere in the muddle. As the magician's magic box with its secret compartment holds his assistant—still there, but out of view—so my mess holds and hides, and hides what it holds. Of course, there's always the risk of accidentally throwing things away. But most of the time, the mess just accretes, acquiring a sort of sedimentary quality, fossilizing what is missing.

Without my mess, I have lost something. A kind of intensity. I am left to keep my chaos in my handbag. A mess of my own. Some physical testament to the fact that I have lived, even if I've lost much of the evidence of that life along the way. As we go forward in time, we keep our pasts in mind. It's in there—among the disintegrating tissues, and the boxes of crayons, and the peculiarly shaped piece of (probably) Plasticine—the traces of the people we have known, lost properties of love.

# OXFORD
## —2003—

EVENTUALLY MY BARRIER METHOD FAILED.

He was a long-haired engineer who looked a bit like Tom Cruise left out in the rain. A completist in all things, he collected prog-rock vinyl, and spent hours on websites about Swedish geological formations. I was invited to a party at his house. The night before, I had a dream that we had amazing, passionate, extraordinary sex—one of those dreams that leave you sad to wake up.

Dreams are not necessarily a good basis for a relationship.

I cornered him at the party and kissed him to the strains of Captain Beefheart. He told me that he would make a very bad boyfriend. I chose not to listen. I got pregnant. It was our own faults—messy carelessness on a trip to Uppsala, combined with that astonishing disbelief that my body would do what all the books had told me, for so long, it could do. Too embarrassed to go to a Swedish chemist, I waited till we got back to Heathrow, then bought a small, expensive, nearly empty cardboard box in the airport pharmacy. The morning-after pill. Known to be effective seventy-two hours after unprotected sex. But less effective the later you leave it. It was too late, in my case. My messy timekeeping meant that one kind of future life had already taken hold of my body. The tidy boyfriend couldn't contemplate the thought of the chaos a child would bring to his world, and when he spoke about the inconvenience and expense of it all, I realized I couldn't contemplate the thought of entangling my life with his.

In the abortion clinic I glanced at the screen. It was turned away from me so I saw nothing but a faint haze of black and white, but I was left with an imagined image of a kind of alien tadpole floating inside me against a background of outer space. I was admitted as a day patient to the hospital, where they gave me another, stronger kind of pill, one designed to abort, and a cardboard container to take with me every time I went to the toilet cubicle, which I was to leave in the toilet pan. I wondered who had the job of inspecting this mess of blood, piss, and clumps of tissue.

Back in my two rooms, I crawled onto my foam sofa bed, an invalid without a cause, undeserving of grapes or flowers. The boyfriend said he was exhausted by his day as a father-not-to-be, and—in the absence of a chair—lay down beside me. He seemed, at that moment, like so much matter out of place.

I don't know where he is now. I think married. I hope happy. But he rarely crosses my mind. I sometimes think of that mess in the cardboard tray, though. How life would have changed, off these rails, onto another track.

# MOSCOW TO
# ST. PETERSBURG

LENINGRADSKY STATION IS NO CALMER TODAY THAN IT would have been for Anna. The building still glows with illuminated strips at the bottom of its windows, turning the snow on the grubby concourse an unpleasant shade of artificial yellow. Passengers still run from taxis, up the station steps, slamming car boots, remembering, forgetting, remembering again. The central station tower does not quite win over the neighboring metro, with its cupola and spire, but it jostles against it, in a spirit of solid competition. The four-sided railway clock looks down reproachfully. No escaping Moscow time. Walking inside, the enormous departure board blurs, a line of black and gray. People move forward with their bags, past pickpockets in black jackets framing the doorway, finding themselves faced with the large white-edged clock hanging above the main hall. Anyone can be in St. Petersburg in four hours straight on the day train.

The shiny granite concourse opens out into the atrium. Everywhere the screens and arrows point you forward. The concourse and shopping mall are crowded with coffee stalls and mobile-phone-cover stands, and ranks of curved red seats. Beyond them are the security checks, people queuing to place their bags on the conveyor, shoving their worldly goods in through the vinyl fringe, to disappear temporarily, like coffins heading for the furnace.

The trains that run the Moscow to Petersburg line seem to have a life of their own. Always the trains wait, running to time like the vehicular equivalent of a row of grim reapers. Those collections of engines, those timetables, those lines speak to us of the journeys we might take, the other lives we might begin, but also the choices we must make. We cannot ride more than one train at a time.

Walking up to the sleeper train itself is like entering a strange double world. The train is gray and red, the ubiquitous sleek-nosed metal bullet. But the attendants, standing by each door in their red uniforms, seem to come from an earlier time. Stepping up into the carriage, with its red swirled carpets and neatly pelmeted curtains, it is as if the furnishings are yearning, ever so quietly, for the age of steam. The two-bunk carriage is small and neat. The fake samovar cups are placed on each side of the table, a teabag wedged within. A print on the wall is a porthole to the nineteenth century. Even the complimentary chocolate bar looks backward—its wrapper bears a picture of a steam locomotive, conjuring for the daily commuter or the tourist an image of a grander Russia, the Russia of balls in the Winter Palace and high society steeplechases and white-tie operas. A train journey is inherently nostalgic. There's something about this machine powering us forward that makes us think of the way things used to be. As they move forward to their destination, trains take us backward in time.

Anna left Moscow in a hurry. Something had happened the night before, the way that somethings do. She had gone to a ball, impossibly beautiful in a low-necked black velvet dress. Her arms were like ivory, her hair delicately escaping in tendrils down her perfect neck. People watched the dances, waiting to be claimed. She was not the youngest there. She was not even the most conventionally beautiful of women.

77

(In his first drafts, Tolstoy made Anna ungainly, overweight, *jolie laide*.) But even here, on the finished page, she was not expected to be the head turner at that particular dance. Still, everyone noticed her, glancing as she walked in, watching the movement of her head and hands, watching her smile. Everyone, especially Count Alexey Kirillovich Vronsky, a young soldier, a gallant, a man about town. Nothing happened to speak of. Some people at the ball danced with some other people. There was gossip, and cards, and planning. And Anna Karenina danced a mazurka with Alexey Vronsky.

It happened that night—that crackle of electricity between two people, when a possibility emerges, and an imaginary door opens. Something crossed her mind.

But it's about a body as well as a mind. If you say goodbye on a sidewalk, there can be all the static crackle you like. You can feel it, imagine it, know it could have happened, know from their smile, as your heart beats faster. But it hasn't. Nothing can be said to have happened, until one of you touches the other. It can be an accidental touch. The holding out of a hand to help someone from a car, or the brush of one hand against another, to help with a bag. A foot under the table. The taking of a hand in a dance. A hand in a hand, a hand on a waist. The heat of a stranger.

Anna sends a telegram to her husband the very next morning, as if trying to forget. She is coming home. Packing her bag, she feels almost as if she is about to start crying. She bends her face over the tiny handbag, flushed with emotions. Is she herself or someone else. Everything is overflow. And as she fills the bag, her eyes keep filling with tears. Anna felt in that night, and in that moment itself, the solid foundations of her happy family being shaken. All happy families are alike. But now she was different. It was as if, for a moment, she had got on the wrong line and suddenly decided that she rather liked the view. A world she'd never questioned before was at risk.

Later that day, she enters the station by carriage, climbing down in her fur-trimmed traveling coat, handing her smaller bags to her maid. Her brother, Stepan, tipsy from champagne, directs the coachman handing down the larger bags and trunks. Porters are crisscrossing with trolleys of suitcases and blankets. In the background, a mother and daughter are rushing toward the platform, where the lamps shine through the steam of the trains, which wait, chafing and bridling like the horses at their stands. At the platform, her brother is irritating her by standing in front of the entrance to the railway carriage, talking about his dinner. She listens with half an ear. His conversation is not enough to keep her mind from wandering back to the previous night—to that night, to the ball, to the possibility, to his touch.

Tolstoy hated trains. *The railroad is to travel as a whore is to love*, he wrote to a friend. But he was a trainspotter all the same. He noticed the way a passenger looked out of the train window or met another's eyes. He looked at the quality of people's baggage (he made shoes in his spare time), and collected the fragments of conversation that rose above the roar of the engine. The lines of steam run through his books—the bells and the comings and goings, the strangers meeting on the train, an eye for the little things that speak volumes.

In the beginning, trains are just things to play at. Anna's nieces and nephews, playing trains and conductors, with tickets and cardboard boxes, tumble and shout and wave imaginary flags. Later, Anna's son plays trains with a bench and an uncle. These are games that soon turn sour, foreshadowing grief to come.

Anna's relief as the door slams is like the hiss of steam from the engine, as if, in getting on the train and closing the door, she has shut out that other world—the world of other times that she first encountered at the ball. She's heading home at last. Now her good accustomed Petersburg life will go on, as if nothing has happened—just as it always was. She readies herself for the journey in her allotted space, as you might ready yourself for a red-eye flight, with deliberate care and a specific kind of pleasure. Her small hands deftly unlock her small red bag. She takes out a small cushion (everything is travel-sized) and locks up the bag. She wraps her feet with a traveling blanket to keep them warm, then sits down on her reclining fauteuil. It is a crowded carriage for a night journey, and she eyes the large lady opposite her, near the passage, and the invalid at the window, hoping they won't cough too much, or be noisy. She feels on edge.

Train travel, in Anna Karenina's time, was a risky business. Accidents aside, regular travelers were liable to shred their nerves, doctors said, and jar their brains. The Railway Passengers Assurance Company offered varying rates for loss of limbs, eyes, total or partial disablement, or death, which can't have helped anyone's confidence. People thought that trains distorted thoughts, that they disturbed the mind. They thought that they changed the way we feel for the worse. Women, especially, might suffer from all those vibrations. For some, the vibrations were the whole point. A book with tips for those who wanted to get the full effect advised leaning forward—but if no train was nearby, a sewing machine might provide a useful alternative. It's no surprise that the very earliest film of a kiss happens on a train.

It is an awkward attempt at luxury. The bumps and creaks of the night train experience are padded and smoothed over like the stuffed brocade seats, like a smile on a bad conscience. Anna's maid hands her the portable reading lamp, a strange tin contraption that folds up to the size of a lunch box. She opens her smaller handbag and pulls out that English novel and a paper knife for the uncut pages, feeling the movement of the train over the tracks.

Anna begins to read. It is, let us imagine, about eight o'clock in the evening, give or take.

Time, of course, is what it's all about. Traveling by train puts us into a peculiar relationship with time's everyday beat. Trains are not so much time capsules as capsules that keep us apart from time. This goes both ways. If you're trying to avoid getting home in time to cook the fish fingers, then accidentally getting on the stopping service from London to Oxford via Tilehurst and Didcot Parkway is a lucky break. If you're late for a job interview, it's a kind of hell. Sitting there, flicking through your notes, checking your watch, the names of each station ring in your ear like plangent omens. Goring & Streatley, Pangbourne, Twyford, Maidenhead.

And while we're kept apart from the timeline of everyday life, we are forced into an intimate world of space and time with a group of complete strangers. The shared time of trains is understood in silence. We acknowledge it only in our common movements—that posture of edgy anticipation as we lean forward on the platform, our bodies twisting to the left to see if the delayed train has somehow miraculously appeared—and in the quiet collective sigh when a train stops, then starts, then stops again, in the acknowledgment that we, on this train, on this day, are at the mercy of another kind of clock. Much later, Tolstoy writes a novella that relies on these effects. It's the story of a man on a train, telling the story of another time he traveled on a train. A *mise en abyme* of train travels, tunneling one into the other. The teller is afraid of railway carriages. He is horrified by the idea of them. Trains, for him, mean the loss of control. The human succumbs, and the body begins to recognize its own automatic impulses, its desire and its lust.

Somewhere between Hatfield & Stainforth and Kirk Sandall we enter a landscape of rubble and brush grass that looks like the Cornish coast of my childhood holidays, were it not for the derelict black quarrying machines on the bank. Then we enter farming country again, more yellow fields interrupted by rust-colored copses, and then back to the backs of other people's worlds, this time too fast to see anything but a blur of garden fences and satellite dishes. Before Doncaster, we slow down, crawling through the grid of crisscross lines and bridges.

It's a long stop, made longer by the heaving of buggies onto the train. Through the hexagonal beehive mesh attached to the train window, I watch the people standing on platform 6. People waiting in stations have particular postures, ways of standing and being, to ward off time. One person is leaning forward, pacing from foot to foot. Another is checking their phone, that familiar stance of head bent and hands cupped, as if in prayer. A third moves in a sidestepping circle, turning to look at the posters and the rails, again and again, as if creating a new form of dance. There's a final flurry as the last family attempts to get their buggy, loaded with shopping, through the train's inner sliding doors. The child runs forward into the crowded carriage. We move off. The child climbs back into her buggy, on top of the shopping, and sits majestically in the aisle.

Drawing out of the station, I look at the rails in the distance, crossing like spaghetti, and something that resembles an enormous concrete igloo. Someone opens a window and the sound of the wind thumping against the frame makes us all look up, around, and down again. The man nearby is fingering the table in front of his seat, tracing the curve of three small C-shaped cuts on the melamine surface. The sun is streaming in as we speed up through the trees and quarries on the line, past Asda and Outdoor Living and the factory for special alloys and a yard full of stationary cranes. The run-up to Meadowhall interchange prefaced by endless car parks. Then on to Sheffield. Bottle-green railings and dark stone walls sprouting horizontal bonsai trees and lichen. And the Forgemasters, through a forest of silver birch. Rubbish down the banks. Tires and bottles. A rolled-up mattress oddly like a body.

# SHEFFIELD TO BIRMINGHAM NEW STREET

## —2016—

WE CHANGE AT SHEFFIELD AND I HAVE A LUKEWARM cappuccino. My new train (new to me) is less crowded, but I am near enough to others to see what they are doing. My neighbor's telephone goes off from time to time, making the sound of a moderately sized object falling down the toilet. The sound itself is not irritating. The problem is more that I can't predict when it is going to happen. I look at her knee. Her phone, with its cracked screen, trembles gently with the train's rhythm. While conscious that this woman's bare knee is closer to my knee than is psychologically comfortable for me (or, probably, for her) and that both of us can actually feel the heat of each other's bodies radiating onto the thigh-bit of our knees, both of us silently accept our proximity as a necessary consequence of being on a train. Glancing to my right, I can see that the two men who are typing away on their laptops are considerably more comfortable sharing the same space than we are. Something about the positioning of their elbows suggests that they probably know each other.

I look at my book, which lies beside me like a kind of time-space capsule. Books, like trains, are another way of tricking time, of moving to a different beat, a different space. Perhaps this is why we read when we travel. Books break the rules of time. They can collapse time, and skip over it. Some people get lost in books. While forced to stand in the almost suffocating Underground air, the imagination is free to stroll on a beach, with nobody saying when to stop and start. You might have been thinking about the monotony of the day, with its checklist of bite-size tasks—the swimsuit that needs ordering that won't look good because it flattens your top half in a weird way, the milk to pick up, the overdue thank-you card to send—but the book opens a world that moves in leaps and bounds. A day in the office lasts a few seconds. A five-minute meeting in a café can last an hour or a day. If you could read forever—maybe, just maybe, your life could go on forever. A book can make time stand still. It can make it go backward. And there is a kind of arousal to all of this. It can be thrilling to be in control of our own time. As a reader, you can read slowly. Turn back, hold back, keep the climax at bay. And no amount of clock time can stop us from doing this. Time, and pleasure, are in our hands.

Trains are erotic. (Anyone on the 7:15 to Birmingham New Street may not agree. And the arousing qualities of the rush-hour InterCity may be an acquired taste, if you don't happen to be what is known as a *siderodromophiliac*.) In books, and in films, trains have always stood for some kind of arousal. (I read an article that tells me traveling by train can alter the body's chemistry.) A train carriage is a forcing-house for the idea of sex, as one Edwardian heroine puts it.

So *reading* on trains intensifies the thrill. People have always wanted to read differently, think differently even, when they're on the move. The airplane novel, the beach read, the flysheet, the trashy yellowbacks. *Valentine Vox: The Ventriloquist*, *The Stockbroker's Wife*. (In that first film of the first kiss on a train, the woman isn't looking out of the window, but reading a book. It's double transport. Doubly erotic. The book is pushed aside as the clinch begins. She is a reckless thrill-seeker, dangerously addicted to her yellow-backed novel. Bigamy and bodices and bloody murder.)

Everyone still reads on Russian trains. If you look around the Sapsan Express, which runs nine times a day between Moscow and St. Petersburg, you'll see them all. A man turning the pages of an essay collection by Marilynne Robinson. A woman engrossed in *Brave New World*. A bleached blonde, asleep, a copy of Isaac Babel's *Red Cavalry* resting on her red patent-leather handbag, an Anna for our time.

Anna is both hidden and on show. As a woman reading on a train, she is doubly disturbed, and doubly disturbing. Her mind is guessable—but nothing is really *known*. She is like any public reader. Nearly—but not quite—in a world of her own. Absorbed in a book, but visible to us, the reader is always an alluring figure. Abandoned, partially lost to us in another world. I cannot have, or touch, what she has as she reads. Reading is an act of retreat, of privacy—a pushing away. There used to be an art to reading on trains. Guidebooks told Victorian readers that the secret of reading in railway carriages is to hold one's arms at a perfect 90-degree angle to prevent the vibrations from the carriages spreading to the arms and book. It sounds like an elaborate kind of yoga. It can only be achieved through the exertion of muscular power; the full elasticity of the arms, from the shoulders downward, acting like carriage springs to the volume.

The readers on my train are strangely hidden too. The woman near the aisle is looking through the back pages of an old Letts diary. The person near the door, in maroon and orange trousers, is scrolling on their phone. Another man opens up a blue plastic carrier bag, looking around himself almost furtively. It contains a biography of Marilyn Monroe. I catch his eye and we both look down. The secret of reading.

# BOLOGOYE STATION

THE TRAIN MOVES SLOWLY ALONG ITS GAUGE, AROUND about 23 mph, then slows for a stop. Anna pulls out her book, that English novel, and finds her place. It's a difficult reorientation, from clock time to novel time, like jumping between two carriages when you can see the ground moving beneath you. At first she cannot concentrate on the book. There are too many people moving around, opening and closing doors, making noises, and then the louder sound of the train grinding and juddering, picking up speed. But at last she manages to focus, to follow the line of the story. But not for long. She puts her book aside, overcome by the heat of the carriage, almost dizzy, delirious. Not even sure if she is going backward or forward or standing still. She starts to feel as if the world is unreal. Wondering if it really is her maid sitting beside her or someone that she's never even met. Is she, Anna, really even there? *Am I myself or someone else?* she asks. Scenes from the previous night jump into her mind, each distinct, each bright, like the paper strip of a magic lantern. There is a dark place that she might walk toward. She knows that she does not need to, but that she might. The train pulls into Bologoye. She decides that she has to get out, to feel the night air and the snowstorm that surrounds her. She hears the *tearing and whistling around the corner of the station between the wheels of the carriages and along the posts. Carriages, posts, people—everything that was visible was covered on one side with snow, and being continually covered with more.* People are making their last-minute dash to reboard the night train. For a moment there are men running to and fro, *their steps crackling on the platform*, telegrams, confusion, smokers. Now, as then, Bologoye Station is a junction. For the twenty-thousand-odd people who live there, it is a home, a workplace, a place of birth and death and happening. For many others, it is simply a waiting point. A refreshment break. An expanse of pearl gray sky behind a crisscross of wires and lamps and railings.

As Anna stands at Bologoye, feeling the air on her face, Vronsky appears. He has come—he says—to be where she is.

When something like this happens—happens to a person who is meant to be part of a *happy family*—things fall apart. Your heart jumps, catching you somewhere at the back of your throat. It's as if, for a moment, your breath has been taken from you. Perhaps part of the surprise is the inevitability of it all. You knew it was there. You know that they are going to say what they say. The shock is not so much in the hearing it, as in the fact that the declaration has been made. You stand at a platform, or hang on the line. You try to speak, but you are frozen and the words have melted like dry ice. You split into pieces. You are left wanting.

There is, for Anna, nowhere for this new self to exist.

As Karenin's wife, she is one person—another when Seryozha's mother. She is sister to Stepan Oblonsky, idol to her young friend Kitty, and confidante to her sister-in-law Dolly. She is Kate Field, in part. As Anna appears in scene after scene, she multiplies into self after self, until the night when she dances with Vronsky, when her friends notice her trembling with something almost of a self reborn—she becomes a lover, with a *quivering light flashing in her eyes, the smile of happiness and elation that involuntarily curled her lips, and the graceful precision, the exactitude and lightness of her movements . . . the blow had fallen.*

Geographically, romantically, morally, this feeling has no home. *A feeling that both frightened her and made her happy.* As things progress, she is even more muddled in shame, joy, and horror. She is lost for words. No way to *describe all the complexity of those feelings, no thoughts with which to reflect on all that was in her soul.* There are many thoughts for which we have no words, and perhaps words for which we may have no feelings. *No single word in English,* writes Nabokov, *renders all the shades of the Russian* toska. *At its deepest and most painful, it is a sensation of great spiritual anguish, often without any specific cause. At less morbid levels it is a dull ache of the soul, a longing with nothing to long for, a sick pining, a vague restlessness, mental throes, yearning. In particular cases it may be the desire for somebody or something specific, nostalgia, love-sickness. At the lowest level it grades into ennui, boredom.* Anna experiences them all. With nobody to tell, and nobody to hold her, she returns to her seat. She begins playing with the clasp of her handbag again. Opening and anxiously shutting it. She feels the clip lock tight beneath her fingers, then open with a sigh.

Anna's book lies, unread, on the seat. So does mine. She wants to live, not to read. Can a book like *Anna Karenina* give me what I want? I wonder if any book can. Has my reading been a way of keeping me company—of helping me through the worlds of nearlys and barelys and the feelings of missing, and the hopeless messiness? Sometimes, perhaps, this is what reading does. I am at least nostalgic for the time I really believed it could. I think of Jane Eyre, who reads in her orphaned loneliness, hiding in a small breakfast room, then mounting into a window seat. She sits on the seat, shrined in double retirement, enclosed by a red curtain, turning the pages of an illustrated copy of Bewick's *British Birds*. I think of my own reading of *Jane Eyre*, as I lay on top of the pale green sofa, aged thirteen, trying to forget my father's death. I remember not just the story, but the tactile experience of that copy, with its tissue-thin pages and small navy cover. I remember it as a thing to hold. I think of reading *Anna Karenina* for the first time, the weeks after I took my university examinations—a summer I fell in love with a man who was running in the other direction. As the end of the book approached, I read more and more slowly. I was toying with time, hoping that if I didn't reach the end, then this world would go on, and on. It's as if the act of reading might form a protective layer around the reader, an insulation against the world—shrink-wrapped, or shimmering as if suspended in jelly.

But perhaps this is too dark a vision, too self-sealing. I think back through the readers I saw on the train today. Each seemed to float in their own transparent reading bubble, suspended in a book time that runs on a different line. Perhaps reading is more like an opening, a dissolving. *You are inside it; it is inside you; there is no longer either outside or inside.* Books, then, could be both the holder and the held. Division, for a moment, evaporates.

I have never truly felt this.

When we open a book, we are partly absorbed, but never fully lost in it. Never completely. Many of us forget, as well as recall, the stories of others. (I am not Madame Bovary, nor was I meant to be.) They evaporate in us, *a vast dying sea.* That's a phrase from John Updike, half-remembered by Nicholson Baker. When we finish, he writes, what stays in our mind isn't the story, but our experience of it, and how we lived it in every tactile, visceral moment. We remember a few details of a book—and those details spill out from the pages to the moment we were in, to the place we were when we read it. For you, perhaps, it is the way you spilled a cup of coffee on your lap while you turned the pages of a book of essays on the way to the job interview for the job you didn't get. For Baker, what was once *The Portrait of a Lady* is *now . . . only a plaid lap-blanket bobbing on the waves.* Tolstoy's *Anna Karenina survives as a picnic basket containing a single jar of honey.* Perhaps you are haunted by the image of a beach villa in the book you read on holiday, which you have reimagined in your head, and have dreamed of living in ever since. Or maybe an account of a *dreaming lettuce in the garden* gets half-remembered on a shopping trip, and a cabbage is bought instead. Our reading life is porous and fragmentary, and often far more self-absorbed than we admit.

I have read *Anna Karenina* twice, just about, and skimmed it many times. I have carried it around and not read it many more. I have invented things in it that have never happened in it, and have forgotten things that did. But reading, like any kind of connection, is hard to render in a true account. For me, most books are half-remembered and half-lost things. This one is in the bag beside me, but it has also become the memory of feeling lonely in a park in north London in July 1998 while looking at a tumbledown bridge. And the memory of watching a YouTube video about how to syringe your own ear in a hotel room in Moscow. And a visit to a film studio and the way my friend looked on a sunny day on a bench when a telephone rang. And a handbag. The handbag and the hotel room and the bridge and the earwax and the phone all become the book and float free of the book. They exist for me as a space of wondering. The book is an object I think on and with.

We do not, I think, get lost in books, so much as catch and lose and tangle their details in the narratives of our own lives. The idea of fictional absorption—of becoming another person, of falling in love with a book—is strange to me. But perhaps this is just me. I am a messy reader, losing most of what I see along the way. A careless reader of books and, at times, of people.

Because being at one with another person is something I feel I have never quite understood. As I make my daily journey from home to work and back again, or down the landing from the bathroom to bed, or as I stand in the kitchen making breakfast, or hunting for packed lunch items that are not there, from the back of a fridge that has frosted up and been sprayed by an exploding can of Fanta, I wonder if there is some vital bit of heart that I've missed. Real love, real life—like a real imaginative encounter—is meant to be all-encompassing, transformative, metaphysical. For me, it feels more like a stop on a railway line that I pass on a regular basis, seen through the glass at speed. Somewhere I do not belong, or don't deserve, or don't fully believe in anymore. (Maybe I'm not on a stopping service.)

The journey has worn me down, but I wanted to believe, once upon a time.

I was six years old, sitting on an orange plastic chair in a darkened assembly hall. A nine-year-old boy was singing, dressed in a waistcoat and knickerbockers, accompanied by an out-of-tune school piano, stage right. He was singing about love and asking where it was, and I thought it was the most beautiful thing I had ever heard.

As Bill Sikes came out of the wings to sit on his mum's lap, Oliver rubbed his nose with the back of his hand, and embarked on the second verse. The sadness of his song struck me then, as now. The words stretched out into the air for so long that the question seemed to lose its question mark. *Where air air rare is she*, he sang. With the introduction of "she," love became the *act* of loving, a thing one person does, not a thing in itself. But the opening lines still ghost the song. Where is love? There's a conviction in those words, that love has coordinates. A belief that love is in a place, and, like a geocache or Pokémon Go, it must, therefore, be out there. For Oliver, stuck in the cellar of Mr. Sowerberry's funeral parlor, love is a thing lying hidden on a map. It exists apart, over the rainbow, a thing gone astray. The lost properties of love.

But what are the properties of lostness, if lostness is a property that love possesses? Lost can be missing a geographical place. Off the map you expect to be on. Or being lost can be a kind of rapture. A surrender. Lost, like love, is when you cannot find yourself. Lost in love is when you are vulnerable to change. I think back on losing myself with you.

Someone I nearly loved is dying.

# GHOST TRAIN

Something changes in a child's heart when they lose a parent. If you aren't careful, it changes forever. Dead dads. Count them up. It's easy to miss the fact that Anna Karenina was an orphan. Her husband too. Tolstoy lost his father when he was nine. His mother when he was two. It left him desolate. He looked around for someone or something that might stand for pure love. *None will do*, he wrote in his diary. *To whom shall I cling?*

Kate Field was still young by most standards when her father died. It was 1856, and she was seventeen. She was one of the last to know. Away at school in Boston, Field stands, still as a statue, in a series of tableaux sketches, before singing "Come è Bello" and "She Wore a Wreath of Roses" to an audience of a hundred worthy Bostonians. Field was playing the role of an audience member, her eyes focused on the center of the imaginary action. She was, the papers said, the most observed of all observers.

Halfway through the evening, a telegram arrived. Joseph Field had died, unexpectedly, 1,400 miles away, in Mobile, Alabama. Not wishing to disrupt the action, or shock the players, the school matron stood in the wings, holding the envelope, and let the show go on. There Field posed, a living statue, dead still, not knowing that she was enjoying her last hour of still not knowing.

Joseph Field had been her rock and her hero. The only one she adored. The world without him seemed, she wrote,

*so sad, so strange, so desolate. Where shall I find a second father?*
She was lost without him.

What is worse for those left behind? (I am concerned only
with those left behind.) To lose someone suddenly? Unseen?
Or to witness the gradual trickling away of life? Slow death is
like watching a building being dismantled before your eyes.
The back wall, the side walls, the roof—all taken away. Cath-
eters and morphine pumps and jejunal tubes hold it together
for a while—prosthetic body parts, like struts behind a
façade. And then it crumbles. When it has finally gone, with
a slow death, you have had the time to track the collapse. You
can walk the painfully disintegrating stairs, the holes in the
roof. You can trace the routes around the house with your
eyes. You have time to touch the wall and feel the bumps and
the grain. To walk among the archways and watch the fallen
stones. With a slow death, even as they lie there, you can be
with them. Revisiting the memories.

Walking down their corridors, rearranging the furniture.
It is my preference.

With sudden death we read the signs too late. We realize too late what we could have done or said. To be told that
someone you love is gone, unexpectedly, is as if the building
collapsed while your back was turned. You may receive the
news formally, or gravely. You might read it in a newspaper or on Twitter. RIP #muchmissed. A policeman might
come to the door. Or someone might just tell you casually,
on a street corner. Oh, hadn't you heard? It collapsed last
Thursday. Terrible mess. Unbelievable. Something in your
windpipe rises and descends and then drops, as if swallow-
ing itself into your stomach. It hurts. You drop to the ground
and start looking for the pieces. Buildings can't just vanish

into thin air. You try to remember how it looked, how it was put together—but it is no good. You go to the site, but you are too late. It has been built over. People walk past the hole where it stood, as if the world hasn't fallen apart. You wish you had taken the time to walk up the stairs and admire the view last Thursday. You nearly went there for coffee. But it is too late. There isn't even a hole in the ground. Just scaffolding and passing traffic.

A fair percentage of people who lose a loved one try to get them back. The nucleus accumbens in the brain works overtime. Dense with dopamine and yearning, the bereaved will try what they will. Mesmerists and mediums. Chantings and regression. Kate Field tried too. At first she thought to find him in the spirit world, making plans to visit two sisters who famously haunted Boston with their séances. Then she tried to write her way back to him, even borrowing his pen name for her newspaper columns. He wrote as "Straws." She was "Straws Jr." Later she got haunted, walking down Broadway to Kirby's Bookstore at number 663. There, amid the high-end toiletries and croquet sets, was the latest in table-rapping accessories, the planchette. The newspaper ads promised that this small board on wheels would send word from her father from beyond the grave. Kirby's Planchette was a capricious ghostwriter, which claimed to channel one's natural magnetism in order to commune with the spirit world.

The first night Field sat with the board, it gave her exactly what she wanted. Her father's initials, "J. F.," were scrawled in a large and indistinct hand. The next night, she sat up late, awaiting the planchette's movements. At first the board simply directed her hand up and down in a peculiar sawing motion. Then, three times, she wrote the words *Your Father*, and it began to talk to her like a father would. The board called her a dear child and began a sensible lecture on the best route for self-improvement.

I wonder what it would be like to read a voice from the dead. The reconstitution of the voice of an absent person in a line on a board. A dream come spookily true.

Trollope was a year older than Field had been when his father died, but he was no stranger to loss. Three of his siblings were also gone before he reached the age of nineteen. *They were all dying*, he writes, *except my mother*. There's a cold resignation about that *except*. Trollope knew the way that death can make a heart cold. He is so very good at catching anybody's cold ambivalence in truth. His most famous novel begins with a deathbed scene—a son, kneeling by his father's bedside. The father's death means the son will come into a kind of inheritance, but the logistics of this all depends on the right government being in power, which, in turn, rather depends on said father dying sooner rather than later, and the father is taking his time about it. The father was dying *as he had lived, peaceably, slowly, without pain and without excitement.* His breath leaves him almost imperceptibly.

Then the novel takes us to the most painful moment. The hero kneels by his father's bedside, wondering if he will become a bishop, and asks himself a question.

*He dared to ask himself whether he really longed for his father's death.*

This sentence takes my breath away. Here, as elsewhere, Trollope is brave. Brave enough to show the inside of another's mind, with all its selfishness and cowardice and inward turning—brave enough to show the stuff within us all. Waiting for people to die is boring. We must not say so.

Nor should we ever say that mourning can be profitable. For Field's planchette board was part for real, part gimmick. She turned the grief into a book and sold it. People do things like this. Grief encounters. Death does that for all of us. It left Trollope forever chasing other worlds. It left Kate Field impatient. I am, she wrote, always so conscious of the *fleetness of time*, always fearful of *wasting time. I know that I do not accomplish all that I should.*

The true sadness of grief is mixed up with feelings that you are never sad enough. That you are doing it wrongly, or selfishly, or theatrically. And it's far beneath any arrangements of words on a page. It feels as if someone is scraping a grapefruit spoon on the inside of your stomach.

I talk to a friend who is a psychologist. She says that we sometimes try to tell too neat a story about what loss can do. We sit in the bright white of her kitchen and she makes me coffee. She asks some questions and listens. Before I leave she goes up to her study and brings down a book. Sometimes, she says, the experience of losing a parent can be processed as much as a gain as a loss. Intuitively, that makes no sense. You think that when you have lost something, you would be sad, empty, bereft, hollowed out. Actually, it can be that, and something else, too. She opens the book to show me. There's a chapter about the way in which utter devastation— particularly that of losing a parent—can lead some people to feel almost elated. Like they've survived a bomb. The near miss makes them feel as if nothing can touch them again. Of course, the writer says, *losing a parent is not like having your house bombed or being set upon by a crazed mob*:

It's worse. It's not over in one terrible moment, and the injuries do not heal as quickly as a bruise or a wound.

But, like a bomb, he writes, parental death can feel like a kind of near miss. It can, for some, give the sense that a bomb has dropped just beside you. The death of a parent can be a kind of gift to a certain sort of child. The fact of survival leaves you feeling tough, exhilarated. Hardened by experience. I know this.

I like the idea of winning back something from all of this losing. My resentful shell is built up with layers of Teflon conviction, and it's been like that for years. I've always told myself that I need not care too much because, like a gambler whose luck is on the turn, I've hit rock bottom. We losers— the bereaved children—can recognize our kind across a crowded room, sniff each other out at parties. We glance over the shoulder of the present, trying to catch the future's eye.

The worst thing has already happened, and we are still standing.

My dead dad stands on top of the piano, leaning against a wall. A trick of time, he is the same age as I am now, wearing a pale blue shirt, with a clothesline in the background. Two years after that photo was taken, he began to sink. I think I realized something was unusually wrong when he took me to Brent Cross for clothes on my thirteenth birthday—my birthday treat. I walked around the revolving stainless-steel hoops of clothes on hangers, flicked my way through the rows of sweatshirts. Then turned and saw my father out of the corner of my eye, carefully vomiting into the bin near Luggage & Children's Shoes.

By June he was lying in a bed in the back room, except for the two times I found him lying on the floor having a seizure. After that started, we took him out of the front door in a wheelchair. I think we levered him into the back of the green Renault, but it could have been an ambulance. Either way, it felt OK. People who get into ambulances are on their way to getting better. I wasn't aware that sometimes people go to hospital when there is nowhere else to put them.

It wasn't a hospital, though.

The one bonus is that he got away from the stucco, I suppose. Set in a quiet corner of north London, the Edenhall Marie Curie Cancer Centre is in prime property space, its red-brick rectangle rising among leafy trees, between Victorian mansions. They moved him there from the Royal Free, down at the bottom of Pond Street, and in both cases I remember being quite pleased at the prospect of visiting my dad in Hampstead rather than Finchley, partly because it was posh, but mostly because there was a big Body Shop and a Laura Ashley on Hampstead High Street, which meant that I could stare at swimsuits and bottles of gloop, or iridescent globes of oil.

It seems almost impossible to square the knowledge of the pain that was to come with my thirteen-year-old preoccupations at the time. If I did not exactly will or wish for my father's death, waiting for it seemed like a sometimes interesting but mostly burdensome sideline to the rest of my life. Looking at my diary, the entries are all about what to wear to Rachel South's bat mitzvah disco, how neat my handwriting was, whether I should shave my legs, and if I would get a merit in flute.

They let me in alone to see my father's body. He was lying on a plinth bed in the hospice chapel of rest. He was pale, long, his red hair nearly gone, and what was left had faded to the color of sand. When I saw him, I wondered at the new burgundy pajamas. Wherever he was, he wasn't there. Back at home, his sheds and lean-tos struggled in the wind. The rented hearse drove slowly up the road, and we lowered our heads in the crematorium. Relatives bent down to speak to me in the front hall, hunting for words. A friend's father started to talk to me about how it would be from now on. Then his voice broke and he couldn't go on. I think, refreshingly, that he was trying to say that everything wouldn't be alright.

They are very sorry for my loss. I am very sorry for him, too. He arrived the day my father died, wrapped up in brown paper, and I have felt for him ever since. A gray, damp creature with pilled fur and webbed feet. He wasn't labeled, but I knew him straight away. He was my very own Loss. I did not choose him, as you might hope to choose a lifetime companion, but I have grown to know him and his ways. He is clammy and demanding. He smells. He has a habit of turning up at key moments. Graduation ceremonies. Dates. In bed. He really loves Christmas. Every year, he sits in the middle of the table, among the turkey and the roast potatoes. A centerpiece. Later, he moves to the Christmas tree, and sits there for days, as the pine needles fall around him. He has no special allegiance to time or place. He seeps into all festivals and celebrations, seamlessly. My Loss is outgoing. Sometimes embarrassingly so. He forces himself onto people I have only just met, and cuts into conversations that do not concern him. He has a weakness for alcohol. I can almost guarantee that at the end of any drunken evening, my Loss will turn up, tearful, angry, determined not to be left at home. People are very kind about him. They are intrigued at first. He reminds them of their own losses. And they pity him. But my older friends must have tired of him some time ago. I think they must wonder why I haven't brought him up better, why I haven't made more of an effort to control him, or to make him fend for himself. Their losses are usually kept at home. I imagine they may think I bring him along on purpose. And occasionally I do. That's when he stinks the most.

How do children mourn when there are no models of grief? How does anyone mourn when there is no shape to hold the pain? It still wells up inside me from time to time with a fierceness that I fear. Nowadays people make memory boxes. They make tapes. There are websites. There are people trained to help children to try to make a story, a fixed place that provides, if not an ending, then a point of return. I remember more of a blank. A perplexity surrounding me, as adults and children alike wondered what to do with us. This family of four, missing a father. A mother, two teenagers, a baby.

At times I tried to create my own rituals. I had a tape of a piece of music he liked, which I played at full volume, walking around the garden at dusk until I thought my heart might break. I was told to stop it. I created in my imagination a kind of hybrid deity—*Dearfathergoddeardaddy*—and I would lie on the grass under the apple tree, talking to it, making pacts and promises and trade-offs. There were no mourning clothes to wear to show how I was feeling (if I even knew), so I chose, I think, things that I thought would get me noticed. I remember being asked to take my sister for a walk and putting on a hand-me-down two-piece red knitted tube skirt and jumper set. I went around the block with the pram, hoping to be looked at. Nobody did.

A few days later, walking home from school, my head in a copy of *A Bridge to Terabithia*, a man asked me to suck his dick for a tenner.

# FINCHLEY CENTRAL
# TO BURNT OAK
## —1988—

A FORTNIGHT AFTER MY FATHER DIED I WENT TO RACHEL South's disco. I wore a black Aztec-patterned Monsoon shirt (part of a two-piece that my mother had bought me for the funeral) with jeans. After three dances, David Clark's friend asked me if I wanted to kiss David in the car park. (Getting off with people at bat mitzvah discos usually operated by the Cyrano de Bergerac method.) I paused. I hadn't imagined my first kiss would happen in a car park. I didn't really know David. I looked down at my shirt and shook my head. In biology the next day, Michelle Stevens said it was highly possible I was frigid.

The friend emails some more articles about the effects of the death of an attachment figure on children. It can produce, the author says, *a cascade of secondary losses. The loss of the assumptive world, loss of essential caregiving behaviors, loss of proximity and comfort from the attachment figure, and loss of biobehavioral regulation furnished by the attachment figure.*

My eyes begin to glaze over. I prefer to be distracted by the idea of a cascade of loss. A Niagara Falls of losing, beautifully. Sadness like a torrent of water running over a cliff edge and into a fast-flowing river, or like champagne down a stack of coupe glasses, frothing and puddling at the stems. I open the other attachment about attachment. A comprehensive literature review of the effects on children of the death of a parent is a risk factor for a host of related life issues including *depression, criminal or disruptive behaviors, . . . self-concept and self-esteem,* and *early sexual activity*.

Three hundred and sixty-four days after the car park, it looked as if I was finally going to get my long-overdue first kiss and prove Michelle Stevens wrong. I was on a school trip in Athens. My intended kissee was an American boy called Greg, who I'd spoken to over the youth hostel breakfast and who'd asked me round for a bag of Doritos. To get there, I'd need to climb from my balcony onto his. The whole thing could have looked like a suicide attempt, but my planned movement was horizontal rather than vertical, involving going around a corner of the hotel block to his outstretched hand, and benefited from the aid of full daylight and a will to kiss. Greg helped me over the iron railing into his room. I came through the window unscathed, apart from minor knee grazes from the Athenian wall. Face to face, after my entry, there was an excruciating (because unexpected) attempt at dancing around the bed, with no accompanying music. We lay down and ate some of the Doritos (which I'd never tried before and didn't like). It was awkward. I was wondering what was going to happen next, when, to my complete confusion, he shuffled the upper part of his body down to the lower part of the bed. Pulling my cut-offs and panties down, he put his head between my legs, and, with the determination of a man who had been reading some kind of manual, started to lick. We hadn't covered this in biology.

I stayed an hour in his room, and when I got back to mine, everyone was queuing up in the corridor for the bus to the airport. On the tarmac I gave Michelle a verbal memo, and she sought advice from the sixth-formers sitting a few rows farther back in the bus. The group verdict (*disgusting*) was delivered to me when we got on the plane, and I spent the flight home in a state of shock. Greg never wrote to me, so I wrote him a letter in my diary, along with a self-congrat-ulatory doodle, reassuring myself that I had established my non-frigidity, even if half the class now looked at me a bit like they looked at Amanda Banks who had BO.

In the years after my father's death, there wasn't a lot of money. I perfected the art of bedroom-hopping. Depending on the bank balance, varying quantities of foreign-language students came through the door of our stucco semi, some-times one, sometimes three at a time. The rest of us com-pressed ourselves, sardine-style. Toys were packed away. Furniture was requisitioned at speed. My MDF bed would be magically transformed, identical to its former self, apart from the fact that it was now covered in my brother's Star Wars stickers. Carl from Bavaria now slept in a bed like mine, the fairy transfers replaced with scratch marks and the scent of Jif Lemon. I watched Ceefax late into the night, scrolling through the horoscopes with the remote control, waiting to see what the world would hold for an Aries with Leo rising.

I read a lot at this time, especially as it was on the list of approved activities in the household, and most of my reading was about sex. Beginning with what I could find in the house on my parents' bookshelves, I moved from the Penguin copy of *Lady Chatterley's Lover*, full of haunches and forget-me-nots in pubic hair and taxonomies of orgasms, to Desmond Morris's *The Naked Ape*, with its spellbinding cover showing a range of arses, but disappointingly tame contents. It was a year before a friend's mother's copy of *Hollywood Wives* explained what Greg had been doing, and even then, because one of the participants was a dog and the other was Portuguese, it took some figuring out. Julie Burchill's *Ambition*, purchased in the Brent Cross branch of WH Smith, clarified things further, telling me more than I possibly ever needed to know about having an orgy in downtown New York. Anaïs Nin made sex sound all black-and-white and cultural, like something I could put on my university admissions form, along with grade 6 flute.

I read poetry too. Initially because I thought it might make me look interesting. But some of it stuck. Along with the lyrics to Belinda Carlisle and the Bangles, I copied out extracts from Andrew Marvell's "To His Coy Mistress," from my Penguin anthology. The poem touched something in me. It seemed to be teaching me not about technicalities, or positions, or threesomes in Paris, but about attitude. A poem in which one person tells another that she might as well sleep with him because life is short spoke to my sadness and my fear. Andrew Marvell became my insulation, a manifesto for my life.

But whatever I read at that time, death kept creeping in. The couple of years following my father's death had collided with one of the biggest advertising campaigns in history—run by the government department that my father had worked for. When I got off the 221 bus for school, the streets were lined with frightening posters about death that looked like massive chalkboards. At home, we sat at the table eating Lean Cuisine chicken in orange sauce with wild rice, bought because it was quick, without realizing that it was diet food. TV shows were interrupted by the repeated images of a volcano exploding.

Great chunks of rock flew into the air. A tombstone fell to the ground. Some bloke started drilling. It was, John Hurt told us, *spreading*. I found an AIDS leaflet in the hall desk drawer. Now that I knew the technical language to describe what had happened with Greg, I devoted a few hours every weekend to sitting by the phone, nearly calling the Terrence Higgins helpline, to discuss the ramifications of cunnilingus.

When not worrying about trying not-to-die-of-ignorance, I needed a way to fill my time. I got through to the Terrence Higgins people once and they told me I was probably OK, but I still thought my number was up. Given that everyone around me seemed to be liable to die, something in my child mind figured I might as well make the most of it.

Rule No. 1: I can get away with more than I think. After school one day, I got off the train with a stranger. He'd spotted me in the back carriage, between Camden and Burnt Oak. I'd caught his eye, and nobody knew where I was. We walked down the high street together, stopping at the corner shop to buy a liter bottle of cider, some bread and cheese, and an onion. Then stopping again to call my mother, from a red phone box, and lie. He took me to a scrubby meadow, near a railway line, with no passersby in sight. Afterward he made us sandwiches. We didn't have a knife, so he pulled the cheese into pieces with dirty fingernails, and broke pieces of onion off in curved shards. I held the slices of bread open on my lap. It was getting late, and as night fell I felt as if I were flying above myself, looking down from the railway bridge on the two figures below. This was my secret life, and I loved it. Years later, I can still taste the bread and the feeling of risk, the bitter onion.

# CHALK FARM TO BELSIZE PARK

## —1991—

AT SIXTEEN, THE GAME WAS WELL CRAFTED. BY DAY I WAS A school prefect. The teacher's favorite, the bereaved child who never stopped smiling. I was the girl who was chosen to read Edith Sitwell poems in assembly, who was placed next to the guest speakers, who looked after the juniors, the girl who always got full marks and scholarships, the girl who knew the textbooks inside and out. And so I was a textbook example of what can go wrong when a parent dies. It was as if I'd gone through the manual of high-risk behavior in adolescence, picking a choice selection of the best entries. Behind the good school grades was something quite different. After finishing my homework, I changed out of my school uniform, took my cigarettes out of my art box, and headed back down the Northern Line.

And so it goes. The one who ran the Dungeons and Dragons shop. The one outside the pub. The one who turned up in our school common room and didn't go away. The one who ran the secondhand bookshop where I worked, and where we turned the sign to Closed and lay down on the floor in his back office. The one I met in the cinema. The one behind the skip. The one with a cucumber. The ones in Highgate Cemetery after dark. The one by Camden canal. The one on the pile of coats at a party. Halfway to Nottingham, the one on the train.

Usually they were one-day stands. Nights were too hard to explain, but on afternoons I could do it and get back without having to say where I'd been. It was enough to say I was out. I approached the entire business as a challenge to myself, channeling Thoreau, via *Dead Poets Society*. This was how to live completely. To *suck out all the marrow of life*. I was less a sort of service provider than a person with a compulsion, my body split into two parts. It was a numbers game. A weekend wasn't, in my eyes, a success unless I had got off with someone, and the higher the risk, the higher the score. Underground, anything is permitted. Overground too. One summer afternoon a man took me back to his caravan on a building site. A woman sat near a hob, shaking. He gave the woman something, and then she left. We lay together on the bed shelf. The blankets smelled of dog.

The game often took me back to Belsize Park, near my old school, just so that I could walk the same streets. I loved looking at the names of the stations, the ones that I'd looked at with my father as a child. Walking down the high street, past the snack van and the heath, just so that I could hang around those pavements, smoking Camel Lights in their blue packet, trying to turn back time, or fight against it. Losing farther, losing faster.

Nothing that happened with these men or boys gave me much in the way of pleasure. Pleasure wasn't part of the story that I was writing for myself, or part of the game I was playing. It may or may not be a mere detail to add that I would agree to do everything and anything *but*, a caveat that often left me on my knees on a pavement or path. I never fully articulated why, but it had something to do with emptiness, and a little to do with control. I would lose nearly everything but my virginity. When I walk down the street the scent of a Callery pear catches in my throat.

Some might say all this riskiness is a kind of death wish. Part of a mindset for those people who resist life, who chase the end of the tunnel, who want the story to end. But for me, the creation of this double life, the seeking and searching after multiple stories, has always been about life—not death. It's always been an attempt to create more—to feel more, not less, alive. The joy of being *an athlete of the clock, bending odd hours into an unprecedented and unsuspected second life*. A warding off of *the devouring gray sensation of time.* It comes from a positive hunger, not negative doubt—and it brings with it the fiction of abundance, or the fiction of more of life's stories.

I still on occasion cross that stretch of London, but I'm not quite sure what I'm looking for. Those roads have become lined with death, and pain, and life, and love, and strange loops of time—they still haunt me, as if they hold the answer. The ground can become layered with the stories we have lived. The topography of nearlys.

I even went back to the hospice. Waiting outside for a while, on the other side of the road, until I got tired of being stared at by the people coming in and out of the nearby flats. A forty-year-old woman with bad hair and red eyes, standing staring at a concrete block. But perhaps, when you live opposite a hospice, you get used to that kind of thing. That pavement full of teary bodies leaning on lampposts.

I stood outside the sliding security doors, and they zapped me in. I knew that I'd start crying the moment I opened my mouth. The kind man on the door took one look at my face and ushered me into the "Quiet Room." I told him my story. The short version.

My father died here. In 1988.

The man went to get me some tissues.

It's hard to pin down the particular quality of feeling created by the palliative care decorative atmosphere. While it can't be timeless, hospice chic does have its own kind of classic status: standing in that room, it could have been any time between the 1980s and now. The purple carpet, two chairs placed on either side of a low table, on which was perched a large piece of curved bark. On the back wall there was a sideboard decorated with a potted plant called "Decorum," a bowl full of stones and marbles, and a cardboard box for prayer requests, wrapped in yellow paper. A circular piece of stained glass on the far wall created a window to nowhere. And three pictures of flowers were hung just a little too high up, squashed under a window frame. It's not surprising that such rooms feel painfully sad, but there is a further sense of heroic sadness here—something to do with these ownerless objects, placed so carefully by an unknown hand, hoping to offer some comfort to others.

The man came back with a pile of tissues. He showed me the books of remembrance, placed on stands on the table in the corner. Perhaps you'll find him there, he said. I liked the euphemism. Perhaps I would. I looked through the lists of names. Death after death, day after day, before realizing that they only went back to 1994. I would never find my father in that book. But I didn't want to leave that space. When I did, I asked the kind man where the chapel of rest used to be. I wanted to know where I had been standing when I last saw my father. Where in the building had I seen him lying, so still, so laid out, so palely dead? The man gestured back to the Quiet Room. We converted it, he said, to make it less denominational. I walked out of the hospice, reimagining the room in the light of this knowledge. The shape of my father's body hovered over the pine table. His head superimposed on the paper-lantern floor lamp. His feet resting on a purple plaid chair.

A lamp. A table. A chair. Objects help mourning. They give something to hold on to, to reflect on. A talismanic effect, if they have been held by the lost person. Perhaps they will somehow allow a way back. But there was so little left that ever belonged to my father. Soon after he died, the folded wheelchair went back to the hospital. Next went the empty briefcase—the black civil service bag that he carried to the job that I sensed he never felt quite at home in but worked at to pay the bills. I asked to keep it, but my mother said they would need it returned. As I think back, that bag was a symbol of almost everything my father stood for: his determination, his resignation, his containment. The compartmentalized life, neatly divided for paper and pens, and a packet of Salt 'n' Shake crisps, with their own individualized sachet of salt. The briefcase sat in the corner for a month or two, propped up against the standard lamp, and conjured up the emptiness that comes from being told at thirty-five that you are going to die. Then living like that for a decade, as you watch your children grow, knowing you will never see them grow up.

Bit by bit, my father's clothes disappeared. First from the wardrobe, then the drawers. The last items were put into the bedbox in the spare room and then vanished. So did his camera. His records. It wasn't a deliberate act of clearance. We just had moths. Or damp. Or paying guests. And as we moved, they moved. Things were rearranged, got lost. Ended up in the skip or the dump, or maybe in a filing cabinet.

One day, perhaps a year after his death, I remember looking on the bookshelf near the French windows and finding a small silver box that looked like a Walkman. It was near the same shelf that we used to keep my father's laxatives and tissues, next to the bed that we had brought downstairs when the stairs became too hard to climb. I pressed play. Breaking the quiet of the afternoon, my father spoke. I dropped the machine and listened until my tears came—first silently, then so loud they hurt, drowning out the sound of the dictated letters, in all their blank, neutral precision.

The loss of a voice is one of the saddest of losings. Perhaps this is why the recorded voice feels so painful. It is a lasting thing, which captures something that cannot last. And what is lost is so private and yet so public. A voice belongs to us, as well as to its speaker, or at least to the air in between. Voices are personal in the way a favorite perfume is personal. They have different scents on different pulses. The air vibrates the vocal folds, shortening, bulging, pulsing, modifying, resonating. They come, they go. The way we hear other people is part of the language of love, our listening for their pauses, the particular way they blur their *r*'s when they get excited, or the way tiredness makes every word minutely, subtly, clipped.

Gradually, I got used to the disappearing stuff, numbed to it, as I numbed myself to his going. Sometimes it felt as if so many things were gone that I wasn't sure if he'd ever really existed at all. There is something about childhood bereavement, at least as I know it, that has placed me slant-ways to loss. The thing about *having* stuff, like handbags, or photographs, or fathers, is that you can lose them.

Mostly, now, I just lose smaller things. Keys. Money. Glasses. *The art of losing*, Elizabeth Bishop calls it. You start with a pen, and before you know it, whole realms of loss lie before you, piled-up absences of things that were. You get replacements. You buy cheap and often. You lie about what you've lost. You pretend you never cared. You lose things on purpose, as if it's your special skill.

Most lost objects are within an eighteen-inch radius of where you last remember having them. Most, but not all. In the finding, you need to remember that it is you that is lost, not the thing.

Stuff that I have lost over the years (that I'd quite like back):

An opal that my uncle gave me, mined in Australia

A black leather jacket, left on a coat hook in a club

A purse (snatched in the St. Petersburg railway station last year)

About seventy-eight earrings, including a really nice pair I bought last month

An irreplaceable copy of *Madame Bovary* that belonged to a boyfriend's best friend

My father's glasses

My father

The exact memory of your face

You

I often lose at Paddington Station. It's because it used to have a very large ladies' toilet, on platform 1, and if you're not a Londoner and are going to a party or an important meeting, then it's a good place to get changed. There's a huge counter, where you can do your makeup, and about seven full-length mirrors, so you can take as long as you like without getting in someone else's way. But this means that I tend to unpack my entire handbag, and extra bags, and then realize I'm late and I run, leaving something behind.

I went down to Lost Property once, to try to find a pair of boots I'd left after one particularly quick change. After filling in the form at the office and leaving it at the counter, I stood on the pavement, looking at the stuff they kept in the window. It was a museum of loss. Each object bearing a neat yellow label with its model number and place of finding. There were four mobile phones. One from 2009 that had been found at Bank, a flip model found in 1993 in Chalk Farm, and one the size of a large rodent from 1988 that had been left in Marylebone. Above them was a shelf of cameras. A 1997 Fujifilm, a 2000 Minolta, and some beautiful ones from the seventies that you would have loved. A 1970 Leyton, along with a film canister found on the Holloway Road. Ranged along the bottom shelf, a series of LPs and singles. ABBA, *Mann Made*, John Lee Hooker. Lionel Bart's *Oliver!* was propped in the corner, holding his bowl out. Orphaned objects, silent witnesses to incompetence, drunkenness, absentmindedness, hurry, self-sabotage, carelessness, worry, lateness. Or to panic, depression, passion, giddy excitement, religious devotion, charitable intentions, confusion. All we know is they have been abandoned. There are so many losers, so many reasons for losing. But if it keeps happening, if object after object, person after person, vanishes from your life, you may begin to wonder what is solid. You hold out your hand in the night and clench your fist and find nothing except smoke, melting into thin air.

I wonder what would happen if all my lost possessions came back to me. If I were to enter the Lost Property Office at Baker Street and find each of the objects that I had ever owned and lost, lined up, waiting. The highchair covered in wipe-clean gingham plastic, the handmade rabbit, the beloved pair of boots, all together like the lost-property version of the Last Judgment. Would having these objects back, neatly labeled and catalogued, bring any form of satisfaction? Or is it that I am now more attached to the loss than the having? And what, in the end, would happen to them anyway? In another fifty years or so, these holy relics, the deputies for ourselves, will have dispersed again into a world of eBay and landfill, car boots and charity shops. New meanings made, old meanings lost.

If loss has come too early (and it comes too early for all of us, in truth), if loss has come in the shape of death, there are times when you will do anything to prevent the cascade that follows. As a six-year-old, somehow conscious that something was horribly wrong in the house, I would sit for hours, every night, outside my parents' bedroom, or on the landing, waiting for burglars, trying to catch them. Each night my mother or father would carry me back to my bed. I would lie awake in terror, until I thought they were asleep again, then creep back along the landing. From there, I would look through the banisters, knowing that if a burglar did come in, this would give us all a fighting chance. I would wake the family and we would fight him off together. I was often tired at school.

The invader was internal. It was already inside my father's body, and it was too late to catch him. But unable to comprehend this, not least because I hadn't been told, I created my own truth. The enemy wore a striped T-shirt and an eye mask, like a character out of Richard Scarry. He could break any lock, slip under any door.

At times, I still worry about losing it all. I clutch at bits of my life that are all too present—my children, my husband, my friends—and I suddenly believe they will have disappeared, or ceased to exist. I have offended them, let them down, brought them up wrongly. I feverishly rummage through the psychic equivalent of my oversized bag—so sure that I have lost them, that they are gone forever. I will be alone. By the time I find they are still there, like a mobile phone at the bottom, or in the wrong pocket, my heart is racing, my mouth dry, tears pricking in my eyes.

I have dreams about this. Perhaps we all do.

The dreams of all my teeth falling out.

The one where I am backstage, desperately searching for the script of a play that I cannot find, and nobody will tell me where it is.

The dream in which I am desperately searching for bags, carrying the children's bags from one hotel to another house, then running back, realizing there are always more that I have forgotten to get. And there are always some left unattended.

Dreams of someone I nearly know, going up the escalator in front of me, or of them floating down an escalator as I float up the one opposite.

But there are times when I am hardened to it all. The bomb has fallen and I have still survived. At these dislocated moments, feeling anything much for anything is out of my grasp. Perhaps it is because I am so busy with my Loss. The one everyone is so sorry for. He is bulky, and leaves little room for anyone else, even when they are willing to bunk up. I have been changed once, when Loss and I fell for each other. I fear the thought of changing again. What would I be if a day went by without my thinking of him? My Loss will not let himself be forgotten. His smell lingers under my fingernails. He moves almost noiselessly, but if you listen carefully, you can hear what makes him tick. He does not run by clock time. That would be too easy. My Loss has no past. He looks only to the future. Whenever I step forward, he is there, one step ahead, waiting for me, like the ghostly image on a glass plate.

# BIRMINGHAM
# NEW STREET TO
# LEAMINGTON SPA

## —2016—

THE CHILD NOT IN THE BUGGY GETS OFF AT BIRMINGHAM New Street, having run up and down the carriage, tapping at the seat backs with the persistence of a death metal drummer. I look at him as he pads down the platform, stopping to pick a discarded lolly stick off the concourse, and think of my own children—and about how mind-numbing parenthood can be.

A friend asked me the other day if I missed it. By which she meant, did I miss the double life, the conquests, the danger. I looked across the table for a moment, taken aback by the question, and by the insight that lay beneath it. The answer is not so much that I miss the danger as that I dread the boredom. As the clock edges toward the moment of school pickup, I enter another world of frequent grayness. The boredom of the cooking, the traffic jams and pee stops, the tipping of half-finished bowls of Weetabix down the sink that have sat on the table all day so the milk has curdled and what's left has become crusted to the sides of the bowl like vomit down the sides of a toilet bowl. The guilt of frustration, and the boredom of guilt. The boredom when you hear one of them calling for the iPad at 5:45 a.m. and give in, in a way that makes you feel that you have, yet again, so signally failed. And for sure, it is punctuated by small miracles. But perhaps I am not alone in finding myself fascinated by the ways in which domestic life often feels so desperately drab. Yesterday, for the first time in a year, I was without them.

I sat in a small hotel room in Hull, overlooking a flat roof grimed with mildew. The schedule was mine, to take or leave. I took a bath at midday in the beige floral bathroom, and cut my toenails. I put the red cardboard Do Not Disturb sign on the door, and I slept. I dropped my clothes on the floor and enjoyed the experience of not picking them up. I watched *Bargain Hunt* on the big Samsung TV, which was unhappily bolted to the wall, isolated against a background of faux-pine paneling. Nobody, for once, could come into my room without my invitation. I was responsible for nobody's health and nobody's safety. I could negotiate the space as broadly or as narrowly as I wished. I opened the wardrobe and looked at the Corby Trouser Press. I leafed through the Holy Bible, placed by the Gideons. It opened immediately at 2 Chronicles 32, its pages warped, as if it had been dropped in the bath. It told the story of Hezekiah's pride, success, and death. The sign hung on the door handle like a drawbridge—and a moat. The room had been booked for me by a man at the University of Hull, and he had no idea how happy it was making me. All hotel rooms are alike, but some hotel rooms are more alike than others. I was in Hull to give a public talk about jealousy and envy, and the difference between them. Why are we so ashamed, I wondered, of envy? Why is envy always cast as a woman? Ugly sisters. That foul witch, Sycorax, in *The Tempest*, who is grown into a hoop with envy. It was as good a topic as any, but I'd left the writing of it to the last minute, working from an old talk I'd given some years before. My heart wasn't in it. I would rather have been thinking about

*Anna Karenina.* I imagined another talk I could give. "*Anna Karenina* at Home," I would call it. Complete with pictures of the places that Anna Karenina might have once lived. The life that Tolstoy's wife would have inhabited. Grand houses then were arranged *enfilade*—every room interlocking another. *Enfilade* means gunfire. That makes a kind of sense. Those moments when someone invades a quiet space, running through a room looking for their shoes or their wallet, metaphorically killing the moment. *Enfilade* houses are not quite open plan, but open to constant interruption. In Tolstoy's Moscow house, the tourist groups make their way awkwardly around the building, reversing or side-shifting at the doorways, bumping into the potted ferns that burst out around gathered muslin curtains. A life in time and space punctuated by others. You can imagine the children crashing through the nursery, playing trains, rocketing past their mother, who is copying a manuscript in her bedroom, to reach the dull drawing room with its densely patterned navy blue carpet, its candlesticks and mirrors. Everything is connected. The man fixing the gramophone would be walking into the sitting room to speak about the broken needles, past the maid walking to and fro to fetch water and fruit, and the stuffed bear that held the tray of visiting cards. Visitors walking through the living room would pause in the smaller drawing room, embroidered to within an inch of its life.

Sofia Tolstoy writes of the boredom of it all. She complains about the *nursing, eating, drinking, sleeping and loving and caring for my husband's babies.* The collection of parcels and the sewing. Darning holes and attending to the children's piano lessons. Sometimes shopping. Toys for the children—some tops, a thimble, warm gloves, a brooch. *I wish something would happen soon.* She copies out her husband's diaries: *There is no such thing as love,* he writes. *Only the physical need for intercourse, and the practical need for a life companion.*

*I am,* she said, *a piece of household furniture.*

Part of the furniture. Parental life is full of it. Full of these tiny boredoms. And how cleverly memory erases them. The waiting in the queue for the infant swing in the swarming playground. The emptying of the lunchbox the morning after the night before, and groping in the bread bin to find two matching slices of non-moldy bread. The block-walking with a squalling toddler in a buggy at 3 p.m., desperate for them to have the nap that they're desperately fighting against. A few months later you realize that they wouldn't go to sleep because they have outgrown the nap, and the whole exercise was pointless.

Boredom, though, is less about what you are doing, from emptying the bins to washing up (mundane though these tasks may be), than about a sudden feeling of the absence of alternatives, a feeling of not-looking-forward-to. It's a mode of waiting for something to wait for. Of wanting the experience of wanting. It has something to do with losing our normal experience of how we live in time. How we live together.

Roland Barthes wrote a whole book about what it means to live with other people. A manual about what it means to endure or enjoy the condition of cohabitation. There is, for him, a way in which we might live together in time but still keep our individual freedom. An idea of *idiorhythmic* existence—the concept of living alone-but-together, living to a beat that is both distinct and communal. A group of Greek monks, apparently, have got this nailed. The philosopher managed it in his own way by living with his mum. He doesn't say anything about living with nits.

Perhaps it is the relentless requirement for presentness demanded by the role of parenthood that I find so difficult, and sometimes so frightening. My children, like most, live in the present. I see this in their wonderful impracticality. Their determination to start an elaborate craft activity involving glue and balloons four minutes before we leave for school. In their ability to spend forty-five minutes transfixed by an earwig, and a worm called Jim. And if I let myself feel for their sense of time, I am required to live in the present with them too.

When I watch small children playing, it seems to me that they transform all the rules of time—all our forward looking and ambitions and plans and schemes—into a fiction, a tower of cardboard boxes that can be felled at any point and repurposed to make a dolls' house. This presentness, this being in the now, is delicious, but it is anything but sensible. It threatens all that I construct to keep me moving forward as a responsible adult, as a mother, as a wife. Child's play knows no consequence. Their sense for the moment is dangerous. It brings me close to the recklessness that I used to know so well.

Tolstoy kept his own time in his Moscow house, and a separate working room at the top of the second floor—oilskin walls, and a heavy desk with a small raised rail around the edge. It was calm there, peculiarly remote from the rest of the house, insulated from the sounds of the city or the children shouting in the garden. A separate back staircase provided a quick exit out of the rear of the house to the garden. His days were regularized by his own system—wood chopping, exercises, writing, shoemaking, riding his bicycle. But at 6 p.m., the cuckoo clock on the yellow wall above the dining table would call the family together. Time alone would transform to time together, regulated by the cabbage soup and the hiss of the samovar. You can go and look at his room. Beyond the roped-off boundary, in a glass box, lies the great writer's briefcase. It is black, with brass corners, propped up slightly, and the clasp is open, as if still in use.

I imagine the inside of his bag is clean, just a few papers and a pen. Perhaps a book, and an apple from his orchard—a gift he would take to the nursery, at a time that suited him. There was room in his life to think.

We flash through the runs of houses as the sun comes out. The green fields turn yellow, the speed and light create a kind of strobe effect, the leaves transforming into stripes or streaks as we move south. It's a bright day, the sort where you could burn without realizing it. I feel in my bag for my sun cream. Safely stowed, not forgotten in the chaos and the mess. Years ago they used to call it suntan lotion. It came in bottles with foreign names. Ambre Solaire Piz Buin. Squeezed out to smell of holidays and sandcastles, of my mother in a bikini and my father with a white hat on, digging an enormous paddling pool on the beach for me, because I was scared of the sea.

My father was a golden man, much like my son. Flame-red hair and skin so white the veins on the inside of his arms showed through blue. Growing up, he wanted to be a travel writer. He would have understood Kate Field's desire to keep moving, to keep walking, to see everything. Every summer in his twenties, he would pack his possessions up into a small rucksack and head for Greece—wearing a shirt and shorts. He stood for hours, sketching the Acropolis. A lizard. A cliff.

The moles were bleeding for nearly a year, on and off, my mother told me. It was, for my father, a detail. A small thing. It didn't matter. Nobody really knew about melanoma then. Or about proper sun cream. Extraordinary how the body does it. The mutated melanocyte cells begin nesting deep within a freckle or mole, minute but persistent, pushing their way down through the subcutaneous tissue. They are anarchists, growing out of pattern, careless of geometry and rank. Pleomorphic, giant, hyperactive. They form a mass, hungry for blood. Then swelling in number, they send their misshapen progeny down the line. Neoplastic pioneers heading for the bloodstream to make new families. In-laws and hangers-on pop up, some lost, some full of direction, building themselves new homes in the lymph glands, the watchful sentinels. They gather their force, heading off to distant locations, carried by the blood, and an unstoppable dynasty is begun.

I was thirty-one when my mother noticed the small mole on my arm turning from brown to black, almost red-black at one edge, and slightly harder to the touch. The doctor cut part of it out, then stitched me up. He sat, two weeks later, by the examination couch. We need to take more out, he told me.

There is nothing to worry about. It's early, he told me. He knew about my dead dad. You'll have grandchildren, and you'll see them. Loads of them.

They made what he called a wide local incision. I liked the words, which seemed both big and small simultaneously. As the scar healed, it turned smooth and polished, matching the ones on my father's legs. I have two of them now, on my right arm, one making a large dent, the stitch marks still showing purple, like train tracks.

I would give my right arm to get him back. And somehow, in doing so, I did. Those scars, that dent, give me something that nobody else has ever given me, something nobody else can take away. A memory of loss. Two patches of smooth and hardened skin. They are my near misses. My legacy.

The train goes past Kingswood. Looking around the carriage, the passengers gaze into the middle distance as we curve round the M40. They sit, glazed, like a disaffected theater audience, spectators of lives that are not their own, watching nothing in particular.

# ELEPHANT AND CASTLE
## —1986—

LATER, MY FATHER TOOK ME TO THE REAL ELEPHANT AND Castle. My *Arabian Nights* imagining grew dimmer as we made our way farther down the Northern Line, crammed into a crowded lift with concertina doors, then out into the burgundy-tiled station concourse. We ended up in a shopping center near WH Smith. There really was an elephant, after all, but it was a small one, scratched, and made of fiberglass. It looked tired.

We walked across the road and the roundabouts and took our choice of four lifts to the seventeenth floor. There I sat in one of the tower block's tiny hutch-like offices as my father worked. I named all his cactuses. I busied myself with coloring, peering down at the cars and buses going around a roundabout like Dinky Toys. Colleagues came in and out. The men wore suits. The women smiled and gave me pencils.

I find myself returning to old spaces again. I walk the pavements and ride the Tube lines, as if through treading over the same land I might recover that person and bring him back to life. I walk the woods and the lanes, up the alleyways, and lean over the bridges. And I go underground, an overgrown ghost of my school-uniformed self, getting away with it. I tread my father's steps, Morden via Bank, returning once more to Elephant and Castle. The building where my father worked later got diagnosed as sick, as if to match him. They tried to knock it down but changed their minds and made it into a hipster block of flats instead.

I found the sad elephant. I'd hoped I'd be able to find the building again with a kind of homing instinct, but instead I stood at the intersection, baffled by the traffic, feeling threatened by the noise and the woman flapping a copy of the *Evening Standard* at me. I crossed the road, rounded a corner. At the base of his building there was a pub full of couples drinking, talking, beginning affairs. I looked up at the windows, trying to place his office, but was met instead by a vision of a hundred curtains and potted plants.

I think of him as a student on holiday. I imagine his childhood. I admire cars that I think he would have liked to drive. I have invented a remembered past in motion for him, built up from my imagined version of a cinefilm that I am told exists but which I've never seen.

Distracted from work one day, with my computer teetering on piles of paper among the unwashed crockery, I watch iPlayer. A family is appearing in a reality TV experiment in which they eat their way through the food of the century. This week it's the 1980s. The teenagers wear leg warmers, and headbands in pastel colors. The mother has a perm, and the family eats Pop-Tarts and does aerobics in the front room to Mad Lizzie and "Agadoo." There are plastic beads and SodaStreams, oven chips and Viennettas.

The show is cut through with clips from the period. The drab high streets with Woolworths, the yellow Chopper bikes, the brown television with circular knobs on it. There is a grainy shot of commuters, clad in gray and serge, making their way up the escalators at King's Cross. Then the program cuts to a scene of an office party. Out of the window I can see the blocks of the City. People are moving to a disco beat. The men are in shirts and braces. The women wear polyester pussy-bow blouses. Everyone looks uncomfortably hot. The camera pans around the figures, then briefly focuses in on a couple laughing. In the background, I see a man with red hair, dancing intensely with a laughing brunette, his arms around her waist.

I slide the player button on the clip back and look at it again. It is my father's shirt, and his hair. The tortoiseshell glasses and the smile are his also. I rewind the clip again. She is distractingly young. On each repetition of the play-back, her arm is lifted up and blocks his face, just as I get near enough to saying yes or no.

Is it possible that my father had another life—a life that I haven't imagined? Somewhere in the loop, from home to work, perhaps there was a kink of time. Did my father, too, find that door in the wall, the one with the fluorescent green grass? He pushed it and walked in. It began, I'd say, in the office, the one below. Or they met in the lift, every Thursday, when she came in with a contract for accounts. Then a drink after work. Whisky and ginger ale and a lager top. Smoky bacon crisps. A sharing platter at the Beefeater.

I've never seen him dance.

We never fully know our parents, even though there is some-thing of the childish urge for knowable predictability in all of us. We like to keep them as they are, in their grainy, reli-able poses, half squinting into the light as they hold us by the hand. There is safety in this two-dimensional parent, even when they're gone. We can imagine them as more committed than they are. Clearer. Straighter. Dead or alive, the flat parent seems simpler in their needs. You can look at them and hold them, without the fear that they will slip away.

Yet maybe he wasn't always there as I wished him. And here he was—or here was his double—sweaty, delighted, in love, moving at double disco time as I slid my finger along the time bar.

# PADDINGTON

## —2006—

SURELY NOBODY ENDS IT IN A TRAIN STATION ANYMORE. IT seems like an impossible cliché. But there we were, sitting at a table at Costa, not drinking the coffee in front of us, and wondering whether there were any words that could touch the sadness and the waste. I ate the complimentary wafer biscuit, as if to make up for it. A shame to throw it away. Two and a half years of near goodbyes and desperate reunions and not-so-accidental meetings. The time you called me at midnight and asked me to come down on the bus because you wanted to see me right now, right then. The time I left a friend's wedding early, walking off the dance floor and onto the last train to London in my bridesmaid's dress, because I missed you. The time we were no longer seeing each other and I sat at one of your exhibition talks, in the front row, and you looked at me and smiled and then it all started again. The time, the time—and the sheer embarrassment and waste of the whole thing. Perhaps the couple to my left, also staring at their cups of tea, were having the same trouble. Breaking the heart of another, or having their heart broken. It's never far away.

Paddington is a strange half-sealed nowhere land. The painted panels between the struts of the iron roof turn into transparency, on a ceiling just that bit too high and too clear to feel like a ceiling. The little islands of shops, the Whistle-stop, and the ones for very expensive chocolate and business shirts make it seem like a novelty temple to a religion that never existed, or a monstrous, plantless greenhouse. The clusters of commuters stand or sit in the same posture, their heads all raised to a forty-degree angle, gazing at the departures board as if waiting for the latest savior to descend from a cloud.

It has little to say for itself either, in terms of grand passion (although its bronze bear still sits, full of love and hope, just past the McDonald's on platform 1). Other stations have greater claims for romance. There's the wet Marseille (actually Warner's Burbank lot) where Rick stands, abandoned by Ilsa, rain streaming down her nose like tears. New York's Grand Central, where Elizabeth Smart famously sat down and wept. And, of course, the fictional Milford Junction, scene of tearoom devastation in David Lean's *Brief Encounter*. There, in a black-and-white moment of painful decision-making, a man called Alec and a woman called Laura decide that their affair must end. In some ways the affair had barely begun. They have sat in the cinema together. He has removed a piece of grit from her eye. They have had lunch. And somewhere, painfully, along the way, they have fallen in love. It's impossible. They have to force it to an ending. Alec is off to South Africa. He is going far, far away. Laura is going back to her husband. They sit staring at their tea in the refreshment room, the strains of Rachmaninoff in the background. The expression on Laura's face, played exquisitely by Celia Johnson, makes it look as if she's holding a cup of hemlock.

Throughout all this, the clock looms over the station. The famous Joyce of Whitchurch clock, its whiteness glowing like a tense eyeball. The clock is not on Alec and Laura's side in this film. Their timing was bad in many ways. They met, after all, at the wrong time, in the wrong place. She was meant to be on a shopping trip. He was on his way to surgery. They are both married to other people. This is the time they should each be raising a family. This is no time, as Laura says, to fall in love with someone else. But in some ways they have something in their favor. They are of an age. Laura, you can tell from the fine lines on her face, is nearer forty than thirty. Alec's hairline recedes into the world of fortysomething too.

It was different with us. You were born before my father, and I could tell this from the start, if by nothing else than by your choice of music and your choice of pants. I remembered searching the internet for help, and found a forum called "May to September." These were the early days of webchat and it still seemed miraculous that a stranger called Leanne in Kansas promised me that she found happiness with Barry in Ohio, even though Leanne was twenty-three and Barry was eighty-nine. I held on to the story of Leanne and Barry in the hope that it wasn't impossible.

You can theorize all you want about the two of us. Someone sitting there in Costa, watching us that day, might have said we were playing out some variant on an Electra complex. They could say that I was trying to replace my dead dad with a second father. That I was longing again for that unconditional love that had disappeared behind the crematorium curtains in September 1988. That I had merely slotted you into the shell of loss left behind by my father.

There may be some truth in this. But still, I take their Freudian reading, and I counter it thus:

With a parent's early death comes not the desire to replace that person, but a defiance of the way in which the world measures things. The sense of time that other people live by no longer matters. Death robs you of an imagined future. It also removes your belief in standard chronology, in the idea that a life lived in time works like a railway time-table: predictable, assured, leaving and arriving when it says it does. Since my father's early death, I've always wanted to turn time on its head, stretch it out like chewing gum, tangle it in my hands and hair, roll it into a ball and throw it as hard as I could at a wall, or off the edge of a cliff. If a man of forty-five can disappear, before his time, then the rules of time and age mean nothing. If a man of forty-five can lie on a sick-bed looking so impossibly old that someone takes a thirteen-year-old girl aside, and asks her—so kindly—if she comes to see her grandfather often, then the rules of age are impossible. Death kills time. It no longer matters to me, because the logic of it disappeared long ago.

You made time to come to the station with me that day, traveling along the Victoria Line, then changing at Oxford Circus for Paddington, carrying one of my bags for me, full of spare shoes. It was not a journey you really needed to make. We could have parted at your door, or at the lift at the bottom of the stairwell. But you came anyway, for the ride, and I could hear the sound of your breathing as you walked up the steps onto the concourse, steadying yourself on the silver handrail near the defibrillator.

It was impossible now, we both knew that. You loved that phrase. "It's impossible," you said, when I asked whether we could do things differently. Could I leave a toothbrush? Impossible. Would there ever be a future? Impossible. Children? I never dared to mention children, but the idea flickered—absurdly—on the edge of my vision, like a set of fuzzy dice on a rearview mirror.

"Impossible," you said, looking into the near-empty fridge and pulling out a pot of taramasalata, which we both looked at with a sense of gloom. We sat with the pink goop and a bottle of warm white wine. Impossible, in your terms, didn't mean undesirable, or unwanted. It didn't even mean impractical. It wasn't even a moral thing. Impossibility, in your terms, was a wall you had built up around yourself. Impossibility protected you from others. It divided sex from love. It divided marriage from commitment. It shaped the regular rhythm, the one that made your life, as it was, possible. Impossible meant that you could work, that you could think, that you could capture images, that you could exist in solitary splendor.

I remember the first time I came to your flat—the awe I felt that anyone lived in a place like this. I remember the studio, with its polished white floor, the light bouncing down from the skylights. The two black L-shaped tables. The enormous diffuser on its music-stand base, half broken-open with a burn mark on the inside, the cord tangled down and around. A box of disposable vinyl gloves.

I'd imagined it would be a place of alchemy. A dark room. Trays of fluids and a slopping of chemicals. But that all happened elsewhere now, for the most part. The messy, technical stuff was sent out to labs. It was clean, almost dazzlingly so. But the residue of work in progress was still there. Prints hanging on butterfly clips on strings from the wall, showing the layering of light and time.

And then your two-door camera cupboard with the cameras and side mounts, lined up in a row like an army of overgrown wasps. The Hasselblad—the moon camera, the large format, and the Leica. A row of boxes, containing light. These boxes of nothing, which could be made to mean anything. These boxes that meant everything.

And then up the wrought-iron spiral staircase to the bedroom on the second floor.

One night you photographed me sleeping. A time lapse of a dreaming woman and a dreaming room, blue-gray light. I saw the prints a week later, a mind set adrift, as unreal as a kiss. I looked at the picture. Did the dream belong to me or to you?

Afterward, I used to stand staring at the pinboard above your desk, with its images of objects and places and things. Some that looked like melting Rothkos. Others were attempts to capture the space of time. You were fascinated by time— the way the patina of time builds up over a life. You spent day after day trying to capture that moment of layering in a single image. Look at this, you would say, pulling me into a photograph of a chapel, or a hallway, or a town square, or a railway station. The way photography can make many times stand still. We unfold in time, thinking we are free, you said—but we are not. Only narrative can show us the tem- poral side-shadows, the way we might have been. You took pictures of many people, most of them were women, some of them famous. It was the way you framed things in the first place that drew me to you. It was the way you kept things in frames that pulled us apart.

But if affairs are things we remember, I have little, in the way of things, to help remember you by. Four books of photo- graphs by people you admired, each inscribed with your name and a date (two of those dates from before I was born).

There were more pictures of me, ones I remember being taken. Sitting on the edge of a disconnected bathtub. A series. My back turned. The trouble with photographs, you said, is that you cannot see round the back. That is where they stop short. That is also part of their joy.

I can still see the way I think that you saw me, stilled in safe rectangles of gray and half-tone blue. It is oddly flattening—and flattering—the thought of being put in someone else's art. I could see that I might be there somewhere, somewhere in the shape of it all, but at the same time I had disappeared. I was being reduced and clarified somehow, turned into something that no longer belonged to me.

Maybe Kate Field felt this too, as she found versions of herself appearing in copy after copy of Trollope's fat triple-decker novels. Trollope wrote of Field, or of a version of her, so often. Perhaps, sometimes, he muddled her up with other people. That, too, is what writers do. There must have been, for Field, a peculiar sense of living in a world of parallels, watching these fictional pseudo–Kate Fields walk and talk, and flirt and marry. They look like Field, but expanded, inflated in Trollope's imagination: newer, bigger, cleverer, wittier. They are enlarged.

Later, you began to send me pictures of things you had seen. For safekeeping, you said. In case your computer broke. Really you just wanted me to admire them. I copied the files, faithfully, into my computer. I could look at them, you said, if I liked. I did. My inbox is still full of them. I remember making my way through the thumbnails, scanning the images too fast, carelessly, as I always do—hungry to find out where *I* was, almost as if my place in the picture would determine *if* I was. Decoding the image. Was it a picture of me, or her, or the one before me, or someone else? Tokens for an image, a book without words. Later, when it was over, I still scanned books of your work, impatiently clicking on the icon to *Look inside*. I would scroll through them, flicking the glassed pages of the Kindle versions, the acknowledgments, hoping I'm gone, hoping I'm there, fearing that even if I *am* there, I will miss it. Wondering if I still have a place in your imagination. If you still see me. When I had exhausted that, I would listen to clips of you on YouTube. Applause as you entered the room. The keynote speaker. Your voice always tinnier, tinier than I remembered. But still I could find a sense of you in the characteristic pauses and runs, in the polished phrases, the punchlines.

It's obvious, in one way, why we choose to end impossible things in train stations. Stations are places of meetings and parting—and the punctuality of the whistle as the train draws out of the station where one journey ends, and another starts. But the mechanics of the station—the very fact of the train—also provides a way to make an end happen. It tears two people away from each other. When two people cannot say goodbye, when they cannot bear to say goodbye, the train makes the ending for them. When the display board lights up, it dictates the moment when you have to wrench your-selves away from each other. It takes the parting out of your hands. It's nobody's fault. It's impossible.

We'd played at it before, of course. I remember the second time we ever met. We had talked and talked over lunch until lunch became tea, and then nearly dinner. You had to go back for a meeting and I had to get to a party in London Bridge. You walked me to the Tube that time. I'll show you exactly where to stand, you said, so that when you get out and change at Bank for London Bridge, you'll be at precisely the right intersection. We knew something had happened. We hadn't touched, but we knew something had changed. We parted on the bridge, which spanned the two platforms. I was going east, and you west. You walked down your platform, gesturing to me that I should stand opposite you, wherever you stood. We faced each other. My train drew up, and I could still see half of you through the sliding doors. Then your train drew up too, and you were blocked from view. You were right, of course. I ended up by the exit.

This time, though, it was real. Impossibility had built up between us, like ether. The impossibility of your work being disturbed. The impossibility of my city not being yours. Your impossible desire for solitude. My impossible need for permanence. Your impossible desire for sex. My impossible lack of money. Your impossible generosity. My impossible demands. I walked to the train. As far as I remember, you paid for my coffee. I still owe you for that—as for so much more.

# EUSTON TO INVERNESS

## —2008—

EVERYONE WAS GETTING MARRIED IN 1876—FOR BETTER,
or worse. A sixteen-year-old Annie Oakley fell for a sometime
dog trainer after beating him in a shoot-off. The legendary
scientist John Tyndall married the woman who would later
kill him with an accidental overdose. And the first virtual
wedding played out by telegraph between eastern Arizona
and the coast of California, with the minister's instructions
tapped out at 40 words per minute. Most of the brides, in
those days, would have worn white lace and orange blossom.
Their mothers would have piled up a collection of silver forks
and spoons. Perfume bottles and trifle stands and ready cash
as gifts. The whole thing was like a delicious dream. Reflections of Persian carpets and white gloves and fish slices and
pearls floated on a rose bowl's watery surface. Weddings were
big business for the Victorians. Presents were a weighty obli-
gation. Honeymoons followed a set pattern. Tunbridge Wells
or the Isle of Wight or Bath, if you were on a budget. Those
with more to spend would head abroad, for a version of the
Tour. Rome or Paris, or touring the Italian Riviera, stopping
at spas and casinos along the way. American brides would
find themselves steamboating down the Hudson River, or
falling in love at Niagara Falls.

Trollope always had marriage on his mind. Almost every
one of his novels tackled the question of whether you should
marry Mr. X or Lord Y. Mr. X, for the most part being the
good-looking man who liked gambling, and Lord Y being

your sensible cousin whom you'd known all your life. But Trollope's books that year took an especially dark look down the aisle. One told the story of a reckless bigamist. Another featured an Irish nobleman, a death on a clifftop, and a pregnant mistress. Yet again he called her Kate, yet another namesake for his real Kate to wonder at.

And Tolstoy, too, of course. Honeymoons were, he thought, a kind of abomination, a disillusion, a hole in the sock that constituted the mundane truth of marriage's reality. When he wrote of getting married he was searching the territory of the happy ever after. To taste life after candyland. He writes the story of a woman called Masha seeking the excitement she believes should exist in marriage. Loving her husband was not enough for her, after the happiness of falling in love. She wants movement, excitement, danger. She feels a superabundance of energy running through her body, an itch, a restlessness. Things are not as she imagined they would be.

As for Kate Field, she only played at getting married that year. Approaching her fortieth birthday, she felt the need to escape the written page, to feel and experience an art that would use her whole body. She wanted to act. Perhaps it was the thoughts of her father, a man who'd spent his lifetime on the stage. Perhaps it was the memory of his loss that drove her, as she tried to get her acting career off the ground.

She did her best that year, from Boston to Broadway, New Haven to Providence, Buffalo to Cleveland. A well-known writer taking to the stage. She was cut down by the American press. Her appearance at Booth's Theatre, Broadway, was spun as a piece of hilarious arrogance, and critics trashed her at every turn. It was, they said, *difficult to imagine* anything more unsympathetic than Miss Field's presence and delivery. She was, after all, *neither young nor handsome.*

It was sheer lack of money that led Field to see if she could do better elsewhere. Purchasing an eighteen-guinea ticket from J. Bruce Ismay's office on Broadway, just down the street from Sarony's photographic studio, she took her passage on a White Star liner to Liverpool. She sailed from New York in June of 1875, and had a little over a week to think through her decision. She was one of the few single women in first class, sandwiched on the passenger list between someone called H. J. Sheldon and J. Barclay McCarthay. White Star boasted about its speed, but marketed itself mostly through its luxury. For the first-class passengers, the run was not so much a racetrack but a sort of Peacock Alley, calling at Queenstown for mail and more passengers. Fashions that season were for black straw, feather lockets, and dresses in cream. Far below the first-class elite, a thousand individuals traveled in steerage, wearing whatever they could afford.

Boats, like trains, are where marriages are made—and unmade. New York to Liverpool Docks. From the pictures, it looked like a floating palace-cum-hotel, with a piano, a library, baths, and bridal suites with grand double beds. Couples courted in upholstered corners of the Grand Saloon. There is, reported one captain, always a Belle.

The reality was a little less glamorous. Traveling the Atlantic induced a kind of nauseating tedium. Field wrote of the conflicting claims of *protesting stomachs* along with *shivering timbers, groaning machinery, whistling wind, breaking china, crying babies, and roaring waves. Four senses out of five are systematically outraged,* as she attempted to pour water into a basin, before giving up, and entering the cage of the State Room, feeling limp and frowzy.

Field was engaged as an imaginary fiancée, appearing in a show called *The Honeymoon* at the new Gaiety Theatre on the Strand. The play itself was a kind of updated version of *Taming of the Shrew*, in which an intelligent and articulate woman marries a rich duke, and is then taken on a false honeymoon to a grotty cottage. The duke pretends to be a pauper, and grinds his bride down with onerous tasks such as wine pouring and folk dancing with yokels, until she is seen to be fully surrendered. Then she is (of course) returned to the duke's palace and rewarded with a fully fitted salon for lounging, and all other mod cons. Field played the part of Volante, the sensible younger sister. After some capering around in confessional boxes, a selection of comedy tonsures, and some cast members hidden behind unfeasibly large paintings, Volante gets hitched to the duke's best friend, and everyone lives happily ever after. Kate Field's parents had, in fact, acted in this same play before she'd been born. The same plot, the same tensions between a man and a woman struggling for autonomy.

After the first night, Field sat in her rooms in New Cavendish Street proudly copying out her reviews. She was, the papers said, *excessively pretty—intelligent and piquante*. She was *bright and vivacious*. She was possessed of a *rare quality of ladyhood*. Field's version ran for thirteen nights. Thirteen nights of being dressed in white silk and roses, acting like a woman on the verge of marriage. Thirteen nights of surrendered autonomy.

The Gaiety has long gone now, demolished in the building of Aldwych's Grand Crescent—a sleek hotel stands in its place.

I went there, once, to hunt for Kate Field's ghost, and luxu-
riated in the feeling of being alone in a hotel bar for almost
no reason at all. I spent some time staring at my printouts of
Victorian floor plans trying to figure out where, in this space,
the old theater might have been. Then I gave up and ordered
a sandwich and a glass of wine.

Sitting there, pretending not to be a happily married
woman, I watched the people around me. Couples sitting
tensely, sipping martinis. Imperturbable mauve-clad staff
revolved around, placing napkins on tables. In the middle of
the room there was a large stone statue of a man in a rowing
boat, frozen in motion, his oars aloft. (Marriage is like rowing
a boat, said Tolstoy's Levin. *Very delightful. Very difficult.*)
Hunting for the stage space, I went deeper into the hotel,
down toward the lifts and the carpeted foyer.

I couldn't find a trace of Kate Field at the Aldwych, so
I finished the sandwich and left. But maybe I caught something of her as I stood on the road outside. The figure of a
woman in a black leather jacket, leaving Delaunay's tearoom.
I watched as she hailed a taxi and then looked back, over her
shoulder, at a figure in the crowd.

As a cold Christmas in London approached, Field's
friends asked her whether she had ever loved for real. She
wrote back cheerfully. She'd received offers, she said, but had
to stay true to the dreams of her youth. Trollope wrote and
asked why she hadn't married. Others told her she was missing *the real satisfactions of a woman's life*. Her response: *I am
misunderstood*. Why, she wondered, should a desire for constant change be read as a kind of superficiality? Why would
marriage to a man necessarily mean satisfaction? Why must
a person be only one thing?

I think of my own understanding of marriage. I am, as I sit here, so far past the moment of wondering, of decision-making, of thinking about getting married, so far into the world of school pickups and bin days and reading articles about list-making apps that will prevent relationship discord, that Kate Field's concerns seem hard to comprehend. There never seems to be enough time.

I think back on yesterday. I feel guilt at my snappishness, guilt at my inability to compromise, guilt at my inability to take time with other people, my desire to take time for myself. The words *taking time* suggest I'm removing it from elsewhere—from the space of the couple, from my children, from the family. I am, as I write this, taking time from the world of living together. Wanting to live alone. There's nothing wrong with wanting to live alone *and* wanting to live together. Nothing wrong with that fantasy. In reality, though, most of us (not being Greek monks or famous philosophers) cannot have it both ways. We cannot have our own time and space *and* the company of others.

People talk of the art of parenting, the art of house-keeping, as an exercise in time management. Picking things up as you move from room to room. Never go anywhere empty-handed. Grab five minutes. Multitasking. Planning ahead. Scheduling date nights. Tech sabbaticals. Gathering up the fragments of time. And *fragments* feels too true. Time is in pieces for me right now, in bits. Snatched. Prickly. Tense. There is in our household an unwritten record of time spent. A balance sheet of who has slept and who has taken the children to the park, who has done the school runs and who got to go to work early that day. Who stayed late for a drink. Who didn't sleep well because they stayed up too late, and who didn't sleep because they are a light sleeper and were woken up by a noise on the road, and who is therefore owed a lie-in. There is never enough time to untangle these debts. Even less to untangle what needs to be done, or to do it. Some nights I despair and drink wine at the kitchen table, knowing I will wake in the night with a thirst and my head spinning. The bed seems to drop from under me then rise again, like a padded elevator. I walk downstairs and turn the light on to drink a glass of water. A small pink solar-powered Hawaiian hula girl tick-tocks on the counter, smiling happily to her hula beat.

Putting the story of my marriage into words—from the proposal to the arguments to the walking down the aisle in a white dress and forsaking all others—puts me on edge. It's hard to write about saying "I will." For any marriage, after all, feels like a kind of cliché. In doing this thing, in saying those words, you become one of a series, one of a long line of new beginnings, a tradable token, clad in white strapless satin. Marriage is a myth, of course. It connects with storybook ideas of a perfect call and response, an end to existential loneliness, a dream of ever after.

You can tell a little about how people feel about this from the way they display the aftermath. Some embrace the cliché, with a large canvas-framed shot of smiling hopefulness and cravats. Some hide them away in an album underneath the telly. A friend (now an ex-wife) kept one silver-framed black-and-white shot on the mantelpiece of her sitting room. It was a deliberate shot of the pair of them dancing, taken from behind. You saw his face, looking down at his shoes, and nothing of her but a beautiful back, exposed by the cut of her draped silk wedding dress. I remember thinking about this display of back-turning as a kind of resistance—a resistance to being seen, even to being seen as married.

There is one photo of our wedding displayed in our house, slightly hidden behind others on the cluttered shelf. Looking at it, I hope it shows that there was something real, something that escapes the Hallmark card. But even trying to describe that photo, the fear remains that language will break the feeling into pieces.

> In that last meeting at Costa, you had told me to get married. I had buried the memory of that conversation in my inbox, and tried to bury the memory of you
> I spent eleven months living with a barman who was training to be a life coach
> The barman slept with one of his colleagues in our bed
> I met my husband-to-be on an online dating site
> He kept a painting of an ocean liner in his hall
> The barman's stuff was still in my second bedroom
> The online dating website asked me to tick my financial status
> I ticked "solvent," which was a lie
> Before we got married my husband and I split up three times
> When we were apart, I went to see you
> My husband-to-be wrote me a letter about our breakup
> The letter arrived when I had just got back from your flat
> When I read that letter, I decided to marry him
> The bride wore a secondhand white dress and carried green flowers

The groom weighed 180 lbs.

There were 175 people in the chapel

When the vicar came down to the door, he asked if the
    bride was ready

She wasn't

She needed the loo

My husband came out of the wings, onto the stage of my life, with rolled-up shirt sleeves, a bicycle helmet, and kindness. The first thing that struck me was the candor of his eyes. He seemed unembarrassable. He could be irascible. His kitchen was amazingly clean. His chest freezer was filled with sliced bread and pasta. He slept in the back bedroom of his house, surrounded by books and pictures that he hadn't got round to putting up. He gave me a key to his door and he answered his telephone. He looked past the mess, and the mousetrap in my kitchen. He even looked past the barman's boxes in my spare room. He looked past the tears and asked why I had two circular scars on my right arm, with the skin polished like a dining room table. He asked if I would marry him.

And this is no more adequate—this narrative of wholeness and unity and solidity. I think of my wedding photographs, my brother guiding me up the steps. Standing at one end of the church, I knew that my heart had my husband-to-be in it. It was, as hearts go, full. But it wasn't necessarily just full of him. It also had you in it. And the barman. And that man who used to sell antiques at the corner of the road. And my old art teacher. And the man who ran the bookshop. And the one I dated but couldn't commit to. And all the heroes and heroines I'd read about in storybooks. I kept this from him as I walked down the aisle. It was my secret. All these other loves, or nearly loves, are built up in the layers of my heart. Romantic cholesterol. But even a congested heart still beats.

We went away. The inevitable cliché. The scenes unfolded in the color palette of a 1970s art movie. We went to Skye, an island of flatland and scrubland and endless horizons and sudden hills blocking the view. Like so many honeymoons, it was an odd collection of shared pleasures and jarring disappointment. I had imagined the days stretching ahead full of crackling fires, sex, and whisky. Reading the newspapers in bed, while the rain pattered down on the roof. Holding hands as we gazed through windows. A quick walk to the pub.

A hopelessly interior vision. I'd forgotten to ask what he wanted. He'd forgotten to ask what I wanted. I'd forgotten that he wasn't a mind reader.

The moment we arrived, I realized it wasn't what I had imagined. There is, in Skye, far more outside than inside. This was a holiday made for walking, for hearty windswept togetherness on the move, for early mornings, and porridge, and windbreakers. So that's what we did. We drove to hills and farms with maps. We sat on link ferries to walk around lochs. We walked in a circle then climbed another hill. Stopping at a pub on one of these walks, we met a man who was unloading a crate of fish. Mullet, hake, squid, haddock, mackerel. I looked into the box of shiny dead scales and saw their many eyes looking back at me. We went to an island off our own island. An outcrop of gray and shale. Wondering what to do, we drove down the island's one road, got out of the car, and stood together, on the line where asphalt turned to grass, looking out into the sea.

Honeymoons are the oddest kind of holiday. The idea of traveling together, as newlyweds, is a metaphor—and more than that. It's like a practical test, after the fact, to see if you really are going to get anywhere together, with all of the bag carrying, the looking for parking spaces, the squabbling over the choice of restaurant, and the being sick on the ferry. Honeymoons are also, perhaps, a way of shaping memories. When the whole palaver is fixed in photographic form, they form a way of fixing what it is that the relationship might be. So that later on, you imagine you'll know what needs to be fixed, to get it back to there. And on we sail.

In 1889, Kaiser Wilhelm was piped aboard the new White Star liner to meet his uncle Albert, the Prince of Wales. A little over twenty years later, Kate's friend Frank Millet found himself sinking rather than swimming, perishing in the icy North Atlantic as he helped women and children into the lifeboats. Kate Field and Trollope were long gone by then.

I thought of death, and of life and death, on the night train on our way up to Scotland. I felt the side rail of the bunk bed holding me in as we cornered our way through the night. I moved my legs starfish-wise under the tightly made sheets, feeling the resistance as I pushed back and forth. Barely room to move. My husband lay two or three feet beneath me, wearing a Bananaman T-shirt. One corner of the straitjacketed bedding was starting to give way.

The night after we married, an unexpected snowfall covered Oxford with a thick blanket of white. We woke up blinking. Iced like a cake. We have no one word for this in English. It's so unusual, perhaps, that we don't need to find one. In Russia they call such snowfalls пороша. A pristine awakening. It was April. I was happy when we left. But I still felt the fear of that happiness dissolving, and a resistance to that world of whiteness. I feared it then as I fear it now—the idea of forgetting what has been, as I step into the life to come. I held on to the bed rail, feeling the traces of my past life breaking into the new, like bits of sadness and grit.

# CARNFORTH
## —2015—

I WENT UP TO CARNFORTH STATION IN LANCASHIRE A FEW
months ago. It's a long journey there and back from Oxford,
changing at Wolverhampton and Lancaster on the way, and
an extra stop at Preston on the way back, in rush hour without a seat. I'd been invited to talk about trains. A former student was making a documentary and needed an expert for
hire at short notice. Carnforth, of course, is the scene for
*Brief Encounter*, along with Stalybridge, which often gets forgotten. It was a baking-hot May day, nearly 28°C. My makeup
was sliding down my face, and I could feel my feet sticking
slightly to the cork at the bottom of my sandals as I began
to talk.

Carnforth is a quiet station, down a hill and a slip road.
One of those places where the clock seems to have frozen in
time, and nothing happens for hours until a coach tour arrives.
So the guards turned to listen as I spoke about what trains do
to our imagination, the way they play with our sense of time
and space. Most people who come there are on the black-and-
white movie trail, to visit the Heritage Centre, open daily,
seven days a week—and they, too, turned to watch as I waved
my hands around in front of the cameras, under the enormous
clock. The near silence is interrupted every half an hour by the
sound of the express train going through, or a person coming
through the tunnel with a wheelie suitcase. All the signs from
the film are there, and room after room of railway memora-
bilia, and some very nice loos. After an egg sandwich, I stood

on the spot where Alec must have walked off after saying good-bye to Laura, and looked up and down the empty track. A man came up and told me he had been researching the film for the last fifty years. I looked into his pale blue eyes and wondered what it was about the story's sense of missed opportunity that had held his attention for so long, and I wanted to stop and ask. But I had to catch my own train home.

They sit over their final cup of tea. She in her fur-trimmed coat, her leather clutch bag on the table beside the teacup. Alec asks if he might write to her. Laura says they mustn't. A clean break. It has to be. They promised. I wonder if they ever did stay in touch—if they had been real, that is. They didn't have email then. It's easier to break promises with email. With letters you have to go to the trouble of a stamp and a pen, and write it and cross it out and write it again. All those tiny opportunities to change your mind. With email, just a tap of a button and it's sent.

I often hope that you will write to me. Email, that is. When I sit at my computer, my eye still gets caught by the icon on the bottom line, the way it turns just that shade lighter. It's usually spam, or a reminder about a report I haven't written. But one day, I still dare to hope, you'll send me a photo, or a line. Just coffee, you'll say. Or a drink. x

It will be sent from the same address—one of those old-school email addresses that people acquired in the late nineties that you never bothered to change. Sent at 4:30. After lunch. You'd be sitting at the big desk facing the black bookshelves, with the window to your right. Now maybe you have a laptop, or an iPad. I couldn't imagine you using a touchscreen. You barely knew how to work a mobile phone.

Just coffee.

Is coffee ever just coffee? There's that line in that movie *Brassed Off* where she asks a guy she likes if he wants to come up for a coffee. I don't drink coffee, he says. I haven't got any, she replies. Would it be possible, I thought, for us to meet and for it to be just coffee? For in that act of drinking coffee, surely, you would see the layers of our lives play out—the ways we had crossed and touched, spiraling outward like so much stirred cream.

Anna Karenina sits on the train on the way back to St. Petersburg and remembers that there is a life that she will return to. The life with its familiar rhythms of motherhood, of being a wife and a hostess. A life where time moves according to the expected beat, as regular as the movement of the trains in and out of Moscow. But Vronsky follows her. Onto the train. And back to St. Petersburg. Standing at the tea table, at a Russian soirée, he comes up to her. The samovar. It must have been the nineteenth-century equivalent of the water cooler. They speak. They arrange to meet alone. Eventually—through the painful space of a chapter break—we know they have slept together. Anna is on her knees, literally. She has found everything, and lost it.

If there is a line to cross, as Anna crosses, I have not crossed it. We haven't met since my marriage. We have written once or twice. Come and see me, you had said. Just a thought, you once wrote, though the thought often strays in your direction. But since your illness, it has been silence. I know you must be drawing those around you closer. Your wife. Your children. There is no space for me, for us, for whatever it was that we shared.

I read a book that compares a relationship to a house, with walls and windows. People have affairs, it said, when we build a wall in our house, between our self and our partner— and leave a window open for someone else to get in. It's an analogy that works, and doesn't work. Perhaps it makes sense if you feel that, in the first place, you are someone who lives on solid ground. Someone who owns property. The analogy works if you've looked around the emotional equivalent of your house, and know where the foundations are to start with. What about those of us who feel that they live, not in a house, but in something closer to a train, or a caravan.

Who've lost the property of love, or who never found it in the first place.

When we met before, before it all ended in Paddington, it was you who was most truly leading a double life. Both of us stepped through that door, down that fluorescent green path to an affair, but it was you who had to hide it the most. It was you who had the most to risk. These last few months, I've thought about reopening the door again and again, if only to say goodbye. But the risk is now as great for me, and I can feel it in the way my heart starts to beat faster just at the thought of you.

Sometimes I stalk you from afar. There was an exhibition of your work in my city. A retrospective. I think they meant it was a last hurrah. In the old days, I would have been waved in. A special friend on a special ticket. This time, I paid £8.99 on Ticketmaster and walked in quietly—just another stranger, another admirer in a gallery on a spring afternoon, an anonymous mother pushing a child in a buggy. I nearly didn't go at all, waiting until the day before, the last few hours.

Your shots were perfectly imperfect against the blue walls.

Blurring at the edges into whorls around the figures. Gleaming grays and violets, blacks and whites. Streaks of light and color melting down the paper. A luminous juice carton, pressed by a hand into a leaning Tower of Pisa. A paper bag in the corner of a room, near a door. A doll with its stomach hollowed out, loose-jointed. There was a life in objects, you said. A life in things. And darkness.

Then, near the end of the series of rooms, there were the life studies—a wall of bodies, faces, people running, close-ups of laughing eyes. A series of nudes hung on the final wall. Tiny pictures, the size of a postcard, each developed in the old way, collodion and arsenic. Pulling you in close with all the risk that went into their making. Then a section of images in reverse, printed on tin. Dried Hypo. Fixed forever backward.

I stood there beside a couple in their fifties. They held each other's hands as they scanned the rows. Each photograph showed perhaps a hundred images of a woman, one superimposed upon the other in a palimpsestic blur like a Catherine wheel. I knew that the subject was posing on the edge of a bathtub, her hand trailing into the bath, like something out of Degas. It captured the almost imperceptible moving moment. The passing of time, the poses we take, the many versions of ourselves that we have and play.

I looked closely at the curve of her spine, the set of her hips, and neck, minutely different in each tiny photographic world. Was it me? Could it be? I remember the feeling of your metal bathtub on my thighs, and the act of turning my head to the right to look toward the blank wall. The diffuser and the lamp, creating a simulacrum of morning light.

If that had been a photograph of me, of then, its meaning was no longer legible. Was it a message—a signal sent as a work of art by one person who can no longer speak to the other? A message that you were thinking of me? That you had something to say? That what we shared still mattered? That something had been achieved? Or was it simply a picture. Something finished, something over. Not so much a last word as a thing to fill a gap. It was hard to tell. The layering of bodies, of time in action, made it hard to unravel myself from any of the others who might have passed through that room. The hair looked different from mine, as if it had more curl. The waist was thinner. The neck longer.

Then again, do we ever know what we look like to others?

Can we ever see ourselves from behind?

Perhaps it was just a photograph of someone else's back, an image of turning away. Perhaps it came from long before we met. Or afterward. We all imagine ourselves, in some way, as the one and only. But perhaps, after all, I was simply part of a series, one of many lovers, or imagined lovers, lying, one on top of the other, superimposed like one of those early photographs by Eadweard Muybridge, an endless moving graphic, a palimpsest.

It is a strange feeling, being caught by someone else's eye or pen. Frozen in time, I have always felt smaller and drier in your images, caught in an empty box, then reduced and clarified by light and print. We are all, I suppose, what other people make us—translated, more or less kindly, into something else. Your pictures were always the same. A reflection of what had happened, caught in a lightbox, shaded in grays and mauves, to suit your will. It is tiring being a muse. I am enjoying reversing the process. Turning your pictures into words. I like transforming you—for a while—into a negative of yourself, turning your lights to shade. I distort and bend the truth, molding it in my imagination to create a story that makes sense to me.

And even that is not enough. It is a relief, after it all, to shake myself free from your images. To turn the camera on myself. This is what Sofia Tolstoy did in the end. In a box at Yasnaya Polyana they found her life's work. A box of over a thousand photographs, silver gelatin, taken on a wooden Kodak bellows plate. She kept many and threw away lots more. I wish I could see her mistakes. The things we throw away are often the most revealing.

Midway through his book about time and space, and Greek monks, Roland Barthes looks out of his window and sees a mother, pushing a pram or buggy (the translator calls it a *stroller*) and holding her child by the hand. He talks about the whole scenario—the mother, the child, the contraption that people use to push children along, rather as an anthropologist might if they were making some kind of documentary about interesting visitors from another planet. The scene is a spectacle for him, not a daily truth. The mother is walking *at her own pace, imperturbably*. The child *is being pulled, dragged along*. The mother seems oblivious to the child, and to the child's own life in time.

I couldn't live with Barthes. Not that, I think, he'd want to live with me. He doesn't get it. It's as if he thinks he's the only one to notice that the pair on the pavement are out of sync. This woman, who used to walk past the flat where he lived and wrote all his life, was all too aware of the disparity in speed and leg length between herself and this child (we do not know, of course, that it was her child). Nobody who has accompanied a small person along a pavement in a hurry can overlook the way a long adult arm and a small child's arm fail to find a rhythmic consensus, that awkward regripping of hand in hand, as neither party is able to get it right. But perhaps this woman was late. Or angry, or just fed up. Maybe she was going to buy something to eliminate *les poux*. Is it wrong that when I read this, I spend my time thinking not only of the child-victim, but of the tired woman-also-victim. Perhaps the child has just had a tantrum. Or perhaps they've had to stop in a public toilet because it needed to do an enormous and long-awaited poo. Perhaps she is hurrying because she has to get to the nursery, which is closing in three minutes, to pick up the other passenger for the empty not-really-a-stroller. Perhaps she resents the fact that it's always her that has to do the school run. Perhaps she is running to visit a dying parent. Or a lover. Perhaps she was married to Cyril Connolly.

I turned away from the row of pictures and glanced down at my daughter—and noticed the time. Always the time, moving forward in one direction. I needed to get home, to empty the washing machine, to defrost the chicken, to be a mother. Making my way out of the exhibition, past the smiling lady at the door, I wheeled my not-stroller up the side streets, then along Cornmarket past Debenhams, and waited for the bus. All around me on the pavement the road seemed full of gray-blue bodies, walking like photographic stills come to life. For a moment, through the double glass doors of the buses, I thought I saw you, coming out of a shop door with a red carrier bag in your hand. As I fished out the change for the bus from the bottom of my purse, I looked down. Looking up again, I lost sight of the shop and the door person who wasn't you, behind a sea of Spanish tourists wearing orange rucksacks, following a woman holding a beacon umbrella aloft, like the Statue of Liberty.

Later that afternoon, at school pickup time, I walked out to the street to find the car. The streetlights were turning on down the road, and I could hear the sound of a dog barking from inside a house.

If I went to find you, it really would be the last time—I knew. Perhaps there was one last thing you wanted to tell me. An impossibly small, but impossibly important thing. I thought through my plans for tomorrow. It would be easy enough, I supposed, to find a way. My daughter could go for an extra morning at nursery. My son would be at school. There was a meeting I could move. If I got the 10:30, I could be in Paddington by 11:28. I would email you and you would come to meet me—a disheveled mess of coats and jumpers and cameras and love. It would be like no time had passed at all—as if you had just left the room and walked back in again. We would have lunch in that terrible pub near the back of the station—the one we went to that day it poured with rain. We couldn't go back to yours anymore. But maybe we could sit in the back of a taxi, and I could listen to your voice again, one more time. You would be waiting at the barrier, and as I came through you would greet me with a kiss, and I would get to look again at a face that I had studied so many times—in photographs before I'd even met you, and again whenever I wished, at the click of a button. You would tell me about your pictures. Of the shades of black and the way you could catch the light and frame a scene. You would ask if I was happy. Does he deserve you, you would ask? You would tell me of friends who had died, people I should have known and met. Perhaps you would tell me about other lovers, the way you always did, in a peculiar and successful attempt to make me jealous to no end. Would we talk of dying? Oh, *there will be dying*. There will always be dying.

I thought about it all as I got into the car. I strapped in my daughter and turned on the ignition. The pub, the food, the train. The journey to see you again was so clear in my head, so free and easy that I was almost there beside you. I would wear my silky dress, the short one, and boots, and my leather jacket. If I stuck the dress on a fast wash, along with a pair of tights, it would be dry by the morning. Perhaps, as we sat there, you would ask about my children. Tell me their names, you might ask. Tell me about them. Let me see a picture. There is nothing more important than family, you always said. Nothing.

Somewhere, very quietly, almost as if out of thin air, I heard my daughter's voice. I wondered why the road ahead was so very dark, as if we were passing through a tunnel. I flicked the switch. I'd been driving in the dark for a while.

# TENWAY JUNCTION

THE IDEA OF COMING TO A CROSSROADS IS A COMMON-place. For most of us, a crossroads really is something that we pass through without too much thought. And a junction is simply a junction. If you have a satnav, or trainline app, you know where to go—or you know that when you get there, you are to do what it tells you—although you can be scuppered by the confusion of escalators at Reading and the difficulty of establishing exactly which train you need to get to find your way to Paddington. If you don't find out in time, you might be a little late. It's usually not fatal. But there are those for whom a junction really is a matter of life and death.

Anna's life ends too soon, but not soon enough for her. Too soon—for how could you ever wish the end of a woman full of irritating passion, complexity, and kindness, with her quick movements and laughing head of black curls. Only four years after her story begins, it reaches its end. Her marriage over, her love affair turned sour, Anna gets into her calèche and rattles away to a railway station. On this final journey, she is heading toward Nizhny Novgorod Station, a low-roofed building to the southeast of Moscow. She is a married woman, trying to find her lover, chasing the evening train to Obiralovka, now Zheleznodorozhny. It's a journey that seems to make almost no logical sense. We do not know what she intends to achieve when she gets there, but she is compelled to keep moving. She takes a purse out of her small red bag, and her servant Pyotr buys her the ticket. She endures a bumpy ride in a carriage with another couple. Everything, to Anna, feels suddenly ugly and damaged. Arriving at Obiralovka, she finds a note in scrawled handwriting, a careless hand. He will not return until later. She reads this as a sign that her lover no longer cares. Her marriage is over. The affair is over. It is a May afternoon. The landscape is level, interrupted by clusters of larch trees on the horizon. A series of bruised clouds stretch flatly along the sky. A goods train goes by.

Her death is too soon. But it is also too late. At this critical moment, Anna Karenina is left hanging. Precise as ever, she wanted to fall halfway between the wheels of the front car, but she cannot let go—or something holds on to her. *Her little red handbag which she began to take off her arm delayed her.* She waits for the next truck, and as she waits, it feels as if the years of her childhood are called up to her. She thinks about being a girl again, and brightness. It flashes before her. But still, she keeps her eyes on the train, waiting for the next car. Just when she judges the moment is right—as the midpoint of the car passes her—she throws away her red bag. Almost as if she is about to dive into a swimming pool, she drops her head down between her shoulders, and throws her hands forward, and drops onto the tracks, and onto her knees, lightly, as if she is just about to rise again.

Anna, of course, does not rise. She falls off the platform, off the earth, off the page. There are many suicides in fiction, but this, for me, is the worst. She falls, and at that same moment regret pierces her. Time splits in two.

She is horror-struck at her own decision. Bewildered. Lost. *Where am I?* she asks herself. *What am I doing? Why?*

Then she tries to get up, to rise, to lift herself up, but the iron freight train strikes her head, and she is dragged down under its wheels. An image of a candle flashes across her mind, flaring up brightly as if illuminating all of her life. And then the candle flickers. It grows dim. It goes out.

This is a terrible imagining. It happens not for real, of course, but in the pages of a book set long ago, and far away from me. But something not unlike this still happens most days, all around the world. In twenty-first-century Britain, two hundred people a year step, or jump, or run off a platform. Two hundred desperate bodies, flying, jumping, crushed by metal. It usually happens on a weekday, most often on Mondays (rarely, for some reason, on Wednesdays). Anna is early, then, not late. She kills herself on a Sunday evening, and Tolstoy catches, in her fall, every moment of regret and missed chances and possibilities and waste. He catches the hopes of those who are loved, and who are gone. The moment is shot through with bright light—the intensity of Anna's thoughts, the image of the candle, and perhaps most poignantly, the sudden memories of being a girl. Anna, we realize, is only twenty-eight years old. To be fair, she has lived more than most. She has a husband and a lover and two children—a son from the marriage, a daughter from the affair. She has a reputation. She could have had it all. And now she lies on the railway line, pale, twisted, gone—her skull crushed by freight.

So much of this was invented by Tolstoy. So much of this I invent and elaborate in my mind. But something of this is real. In January 1872, just before he began writing *Anna Karenina*, one of Tolstoy's neighbors jumped in front of a train at the busy Yasenki railway station. Her name was Anna Pirogova.

You can still visit Yasenki, a broad low building in an expanse of snow. If you walk through the main entrance, decorated with its pictures of Tolstoy's military ancestors and its incongruous orange gathered curtains, you will come to the platform that Anna Pirogova would have walked down, past the slatted fences. Heavy freight trains still pass through.

Witnesses said that they saw this real Anna cross herself before she jumped.

Tolstoy took the genuflection, and her name, but added a detail, a variation. In the middle of this tragedy, though, is the lightness of comedy. Anna Pirogova carried something pragmatic—almost poignantly necessary. The newspaper account from 1872 reports that, in her hand, this Anna carried a bundle with a change of underwear. The bundle, the *baluchon*, is a fairy-tale object, but this Anna was in no fairy tale.

Nor was Tolstoy's. Anna Karenina carries not a bundle, but a bag—a handbag that gets in the way. *Her little red handbag which she began to take off her arm delayed her.* It might seem like a mere detail. But its presence here lifts us up for a moment. Its awkwardness, the way it hangs off her arm, containing all that holds her down. The idea of being held up by a handbag as you try to end your life is almost laughable. The flash of color against the freight train allows us a flickering hope of a change of mind.

# GRAND CENTRAL
# TO UTAH

IT WAS A SMALL FUNERAL, WITH A PROCESSION STRETCHING from Welbeck Street, round the corner of Portman Square and left onto York Street. Then the long route northwest, along the Marylebone and Harrow Road, to the cemetery. The mourners made their way through the winding London streets by carriage, and some by foot, a light drizzle in their faces, to bury Trollope alongside Isambard Kingdom Brunel and Charles Babbage. Although it was a private affair, many gathered near the gates to pay their respects. It was, according to the papers, a plain mourning coach, drawn by two horses that carried the kindly and inimitable writer to Paradise, by way of Kensal Green. Rose, his wife, did not attend.

Trollope had married Rose, a bank manager's daughter, one June day, just before his thirtieth birthday. They'd run like a well-oiled machine, give or take, for forty-two years. *My marriage*, he wrote, *was like the marriage of other people.* It's a simile that seems to close a door, while opening up a vortex in its central panel. What *are* other people's marriages like? For Trollope, they are made up of a thousand tiny repetitions. Marriages are worlds of likenesses. Married characters in Trollope's novels go to bed in the usual way, walking up the stairs of their red-brick town houses, putting on their tasseled nightcaps and their nightgowns. The Trollopian day is full of statutes and planning, of laws and gossip, people passing by one another on the street, arrangements being made. The Trollopian night is characterized by its regularity of movements—the allotted portion of domestic pillow talk, the setting the world to rights, the deliberate turning of backs. Living together can be like this—a passing of bodies, a ticking off of tasks, a relay of surface and bottom wiping. We become diminished versions of ourselves, fading like photos that have been too long in the sun. Apparitions. Only last Thursday I was carrying home some shopping when my husband rode past me on a bicycle as if I wasn't there. It was a really windy day, the sort where you are forcing your body against something that feels as if it is pushing you back with every step, but you have to get the pint of milk, the orange juice, and the ham for the children's packed lunches for the following day as the fridge is empty.

And he sped past as if I wasn't there. He was back from work early. I was late. We weren't expecting to see each other, and he didn't see me. Watching his figure disappearing into the distance, shrinking moment by moment, I thought of the fact that we hadn't touched each other—at least not in any way that mattered—for longer than usual. It had been the usual gavotte around the kitchen of a morning. A pattern of bedtimes just ever so slightly syncopated. That absence of touch had felt OK to me. I was tired. (I am still tired.) I wanted a holiday. The timing wasn't right. I didn't want to be held. But I could sense it didn't feel OK to him, and that morning he had told me so as he scratched the thumb of his right hand against his palm. And now he was riding past me in the wind, like we'd never met—helmeted, impervious, untouchable, accidentally, with deliberation.

Later that evening, I go to dinner and talk to a friend. We order an unfeasibly large selection of tapas. I drink two glasses of wine and I worry that our usual is unusual. I worry that we are not normal. She looks sympathetic, so I take out our Normal and explain it. She thinks our Normal is quite normal. But she drinks water and keeps hers quietly under the table, so that I can't quite see it. I wonder if her Normal might be bigger and more frequent than ours. Or perhaps her Normal is sleek and small. A waitress comes over to see if we have finished, and I think about asking about *her* Normal, but realize that this would be inappropriate. I put our Normal back into my handbag, embarrassed that I've shown it to her in the first place. Normals, I sense, are not normally for sharing. Normals are not like Losses.

The idea of a regular sex life can mean many things. It requires something akin to нежность, an untranslatable Russian word that comes closest perhaps to tenderness, or softness. An almost heroic understanding between two people, finding a way to come together, being gentle with each other's sense of time and space. The phrase hides a multitude of complex negotiations, of kindness and compromise and sudden delight in finding that two people might want to be doing exactly the same thing at the same time and can look forward to feeling that way again. Sometimes, though, it means something bleaker. Sometimes regular becomes regularized. Anna's husband ends up making marital sex look crushingly dull. His advances are made with measured steps. He is freshly washed and combed. He is wearing his slippers and carries a book under his arm. You just bet he's folded his socks up. He smiles a special smile. *It's time*, he tells her. *It's time*. Everything, we sense, goes like clockwork.

I suppose one reason why Barthes thinks those Greek idiorhythmic monks have such a good time is because they don't have to find a mutual agreement about this most intimate question of time and space. Bedtime is, for them, a space and time of their own, a space of silence. (Unless, of course, these monks are less celibate than we're told.) A monk (or a nun) doesn't have to explain to another monk (or nun) that they'd felt quite in the mood for it this afternoon, but tonight they'd prefer to go to sleep. The other monk doesn't have to negotiate the sense of intense rejection felt when they advance toward a partner, only to hear them say, not now. The spurned monk doesn't find himself wide awake beside a sleeping body, wondering if he can handle going through it all again tomorrow night.

Later that night, my husband and I lie in bed and share our imagined irregularities. They are often predictable in their form. The banality of the pornographic imagination, the regular well-timed cliché of fantasy. A woman enters the bedroom. A man films us. There are mirrors on the ceiling and blindfolds and endless fucking. In a moment of impossible, physical ecstasy, everyone in the room comes together, in an enormous shuddering mass, then vanishes into the folds of the night. I get out of the bed and pad down the corridor, navigating my way past the laundry baskets, to pee. As I turn the bathroom light on, I wonder where they all would have parked.

The buffet cart glides past, after getting stuck on someone's coat—a tower of disposable cups and Kettle chips, and packets of Rowntree's Randoms pinned to the side. The Tannoy begins the litany. Starbucks coffee, Twinings tea, Aero hot chocolate. Pastries that are normally £2.50 are only £1 with any hot beverage. There is also a selection of alcoholic drinks, a mix-and-match offer of 3 for £10, white wine, rosé, red wine, and also prosecco. The way she says it, all in a rush, as if embarrassed, makes me wonder what the take-up rate for and-also-prosecco is on CrossCountry services. What celebratory moment makes you crack open a mini bottle on the line from Birmingham New Street to Leamington Spa?

One day, one of us will turn to the other side of the marital bed and find it empty. The pillow creased and marked by one stray hair. The pile of books beside the bedside lamp. An imperceptible dent in the mattress where a body used to be. Or automatically reach for the phone to dial and realize there is nobody there, just a flat line, caller not available. One day, like Rose Trollope, one of us will discover what it feels like not to be a couple anymore, not to be a pair. I find that hard to imagine.

The tombstone listed him as a *loving husband, a loving father, and a true friend*. Trollope was sixty-seven years old when he died. One December night, he was laughing over a book about the idea of swapping lives. Then he was gone. No life left to swap.

Kate Field would have trailed his illness from afar, in the pages of the *New York Times* and other papers. On November 6, listed after reports of a violent earthquake in Constantinople and the false news about horse trading in St. Petersburg, she would have learned that he had been seized by something that had the nature of a fit. A little over a week later, his condition was said to have recovered except that the power of speech had not yet returned. Foreign news now focused on terrorists in Madrid and the fact that the Marquess of Queensberry was causing a disturbance in London theaters.

A fortnight later, with Central Park's lake two inches deep in ice, Kate Field's business assets were failing. Anthony Trollope was losing his strength, then critical. Then dead.

We have no record of what she said, or wrote, when she heard the news. Or if she even recognized the man they described in the long column—*an author at once so comfortable and so pleasant*. There are so many of our selves, after all, to recognize. She only desired to be herself. I imagine that when she heard the news, she took out the copies of the books he'd given her and turned them over in her hands. Perhaps she ran her fingers lightly over his handwritten inscriptions. He grew larger in her mind in his final absence. Failings, as she once wrote, disappear in longitude. Longitude brings longing. We hold on to our dead and dying, and magnify them.

Nor do I know if she had anyone to tell. What does one person do to mourn another, when they have no particular right to mourn? Especially when that person's death seems to belong to the world. And even more so when they must grieve alone.

I press my finger against the train glass and think of you again. How am I to mourn you when the time comes? What form could it take? How shall I even form it? I can imagine your funeral even now, in that morbid Tom Sawyer–like way. A chapel full of people from your world, talking about their memories of the versions of you they knew. A comedy vicar. A cluster outside the door, smoking. A full pub.

And it will not be my place to say that I have a small place in your story, or that you have one in mine. I will, no doubt, resort to stalking your virtual ghost. Reading the notices on

Twitter and websites. Standing in an empty playground as I push my daughter on a swing, shouting to the wind. I knew him. *I was adored once, too.*

Perhaps all of us hide our lives in fictions. Many books are love letters. Perhaps this one is too. For the more you look into any book, the more secrets it contains. They open up before us, like a series of Russian nesting dolls in reverse, taking us into ever larger worlds.

What is hidden in Tolstoy's? The stories that exist between the lines and under the covers. But one love story is in plain sight. We don't know the title of the novel that Anna is reading, but it's not hard to guess from the way Tolstoy describes the plot—a woman riding to hounds, a Member of Parliament giving a speech—that we are meant to think that it is something particular, something that might really exist. A book by Anthony Trollope. Not one particular novel of his, to be sure. This book is a fiction—not so much lost as unfindable and indefinable. It is an imaginary Trollope novel—a mixture of several of his works, crisscrossing the plots from his fictional world.

It's not hard to imagine why Tolstoy would choose Trollope.

It's partly a matter of creative convenience. Anna reads Trollope, we can imagine, because as Tolstoy wrote in his study, there would have been a few pocket-sized copies of Trollope's novels in his eyeline, each just the right size to imagine fitting neatly into his heroine's handbag. Anthony Trollope was the English novelist who came immediately to hand, and to mind. But there's more to it than that, I think. Tolstoy chose Trollope for Anna to read because he adored

his work. There are volumes and volumes of the little Tauch-
nitz editions of Trollope in the library at Yasnaya Polyana.
*Trollope kills me*, Tolstoy wrote in his diary. *Trollope kills me
with his excellence.*

But if we throw away the scholarship, and free Anna
from her maker for a moment, then there's another answer
to the question of why she is reading this particular English
novelist. Anna Karenina reads Anthony Trollope because he's
so good.

Before I began to read anything by this most prolific of
Victorians, I thought Trollope to be something like the Woolworths of classic fiction. Steady. Dull. And always bidding for
a comeback. Placed against the passion of *Wuthering Heights*
and the pathos of *Oliver Twist*, I imagined that Trollope's
books would be as unglamorous and sensible looking as their
bearded, waistcoated Victorian author. I was wrong. Trollope is a *roman-fleuve* of passion and chaos. He's Jilly Cooper
meets Henrik Ibsen. He writes about a world of wronged love
and moral uncertainty, of infidelity and human weakness. So
if we imagine a flesh-and-blood Anna walking through the
snow of a gray-skied St. Petersburg, imagine her dancing at
balls, watching the races and the opera, and nursing her children—if we imagine her thinking of marriage, and of love
and affairs, then Trollope makes sense.

When he sat down at the end of his life to write his autobiography, Anthony Trollope admitted—nearly in public—
what one particular American woman had meant to him. *She
is a ray of light to me . . . I do not know*, he adds, *that I should
please her or do any good by naming her*. Field runs through
every one of Trollope's novels. Every one of Trollope's heroines looks like her. Every one of Trollope's heroines looks

to her. You could, if you want, see his books—as so many books are—as one enormous declaration of love. A hidden proposal. A gift.

When Anna reads her book, then, on the seven o'clock to St. Petersburg, perhaps she leaves her anguish behind—just for a moment. Even if she doesn't, she is in good company. For in the pages she turns, Anna Karenina meets a world of someone else's making, a world steeped in the actual pain of someone else's actual love affair. The stories of Kate and Anna collide. Within that imaginary handbag, then, there's something real.

The snow melted, and when spring came, Field took to the road, or at least to the rails. She was forty-four years old, and thinking again of marriage. This time, it was thinking that was done not about herself, but for others. Field had long since dismissed marriage as an experiment that she was not willing to risk. She headed two thousand miles west, to Salt Lake City, on a mission to research and publicize what she called the *Mormon monster*. Field, who was destined never to be a wife, set out to make sure that nobody had more than one.

It's a funny thing, monogamy—no less strange than polygamy in many ways. Some people seem to believe in it as if it's a kind of religion. The idea that each of us should have one love of our life is all too comfortably trotted out. A liturgy with little room for those who find themselves wandering off-piste. Field's problem with Mormon marriages was not so much the number of people in the marriage, as the inequality of balance. Mormon marriage, Field wrote, was domestic abuse. Why, she wondered, should a man have many, and a woman only one? It seems a fair point. (*Don't talk to me about the equality of the sexes*, she once wrote, *when men have a dozen or more pockets and women have none*.)

But there is something about Field's mission that makes it seem as much a personal journey as a political fight. And a complex one, at that. Field may not have been committed to a person, but she was engaged with something—married to something, if you wish. She stuck by the idea of being free. Many tried to capture her. An American poet, a few hotshot newspaper editors, Trollope. But she stood by singularity, in sickness and in health. This wasn't easy. But it had its rewards. Anything, as Auden writes, *which is not the involuntary result of fleeting emotion but the creation of time and will* is *infinitely more interesting . . . than any romance, however passionate.*

If you are married to more than one thing or person at a time, is it really a marriage, or just a series of beginnings? Is it possible to be committed to keeping your options open?

After loading her trunks and bags onto the Pennsylvania through-train from Grand Central, Kate Field changed lines at Chicago, to see the new doll-like town of Pullman, with its straight roads and red brick and limestone trim. She was there by special invitation, to give a lecture and admire the factory works. She spent a night at the Florence Hotel, then made her way back to the station and got into the sleeping car, heading westward into the night. Her car was called Pioneer.

*I have stood all alone*, Field said, *swimming for my life*.

It takes courage to do this. To decide not to form a pair. Or to recognize the self as a layering of loves, floating in water, each transparency laid upon the last. Refusing to choose any one image from the flickering gallery that revolves before our eyes like a magic lantern. To keep steady on your own track. Keeping your options open can go both ways, like the escalator game.

Soon after this, Field settled down, nearly, with a woman called Lilian Whiting. They are buried side by side. Mount Auburn Cemetery, in Massachusetts, lots 8 and 9 on the Acorn Path. But still she traveled alone, companionless, apart from her camera, a Club No. 2 with its special lens. I can glimpse her now. *Kodak-distant*, but still there. I wish I could touch her. I'll salute her at least, through the window of my train, as she sits in hers, surrounded by all the French plate mirrors and mahogany. She is just visible behind the sleeping car curtain now, settling herself down in her neat compartment. She opens her book and begins to read: *All happy families resemble one another. Every unhappy family is unhappy in its own way.*

# LEAMINGTON
# TO BANBURY
## —2016—

I HAVE BEEN KNOWN TO TELL TOO MUCH BEFORE. I WILL probably show too much, and do so in an extravagant fashion. Too many details. The prose equivalent of the dance of the seven veils by a forty-year-old mother of two—embarrassing for all concerned. Confessions are dangerous, Anna Karenina's husband said. *By digging into our souls, we often dig up what might better have remained there unnoticed.*

Telling a story through detail, though, is a way of avoiding other stories. Fixing on one thing can be a way of avoiding something else. Avoiding being fully present. Maybe I like things more than people. Maybe people remind me of death.

Detail: I am a lover of small things—and of clutter. I mind the gap. I could go on and on, looking at the fly on the strip light of the train, the way a fan moves a paper, the print on the carpet, the shadow that is made on the wall where the carriages join, the way you felt about shadows like this, until the quest for reality becomes a kind of madness. As I move forward in a line of thought, the details to the left and the right distract and call to me. And the details of the self. The navel-gazing details. I have a weakness for them too.

Or a strength. Any attempt to sort life into a scale of mattering depends on who is doing the sorting. What, after all, is too small? Do we have to stick to one kind of story? Sometimes, perhaps, we are surprised that a certain kind of person is speaking or writing at all. This is something Tolstoy knew. Perhaps his wife Sofia knew it even more.

There is meaning in those defiantly elaborate doodles that we make when we hang on a phoneline to a dominating speaker. (Detail: Nabokov's wife, Véra, carried a loaded gun in her handbag.)

The unnoticed has a claim. Giving voice to the details can be an act of resistance. Embarrassment is a powerful hinge. It burdens the listener as much as the teller. It makes others conscious of worlds we would rather forget. It is Maggie Nelson's wielding of the personal in public. It is *consenting not to be a single being*.

Which single being can police the riches of embarrassment I have to share? What is my soul, if not common ground to cultivate, fertilize, farm, capitalize? For some, there's only the soul left to dig. Whatever else there was has been removed. (Detail: Tolstoy writes about how men sell off things that belong to women. Anna's brother does it. A whole forest. The lost properties of love.)

Besides, the categories of public and personal are volatile. The boundaries are often arbitrary, often drawn by others. You are directed toward the laws of discretion as if into a lifeboat, but they can sink you. Women and children first.

I am beginning to float away, to create my own private public museum. Opening my bag. Exhibitionism. I curate the details of my inner world. My Loss drives me on, tapping one damp webbed foot on the ground, leaning over my shoulder, making sure that he gets enough space. He adjusts his skin, which falls in folds around the back of his neck, so thin in places that it is almost translucent. He must be seen. He must always be center stage. He has no shame. But this is all my own work.

I keep a note in my purse, written on the back of a receipt for a taxi I shouldn't have taken to I can't remember where. I usually forget I have it and pull it out by accident when I'm looking for something else, and its accidental discovery reminds me of something I can't quite put into words.

The first half reads, in a rollerball scrawl, "I think I left the iron on." The ink gives out here and there, and there's a small smudge toward the end, caused by the shiny surface. I never iron, except when we are about to go to an important occasion like the one we were at when I wrote this—a friend's wedding. I had ironed my top on a low setting, then gone to make a cup of tea. I had almost definitely turned it off. I even remember the unplugging bit, and the placing of the snaky cord back on the board. But my mind began that loop of anxiety again, and was now circulating round the scenario like a hamster on a deadline, exacerbated by the fact that the bride was coming down the aisle, making it difficult to dash back to the church door in the other direction to phone our neighbor (who would probably be out anyway, and besides which I don't think he had our spare keys, as I'd borrowed them back when I last locked myself out and forgotten to return them).

The bride was smiling broadly, beautiful in strapless satin (no bolero), a troupe of bridesmaids in a range of sizes following her. She was leaning on her stepfather's arm and looking from side to side at the congregation, who were leaning out at a thirty-degree angle, to glimpse the wave of white. The church was heavy with the scent of jasmine and eucalyptus. No pew or appliqué banner was left untrimmed. The groom shifted awkwardly from foot to foot as he tried to time when he should turn his head at the right moment, as practiced in the wedding rehearsal.

We were probably not the only couple who felt ourselves hold hands as the about-to-be-newlyweds exchanged their vows. I could see in the pew ahead, and in the one diagonally opposite, other pairs of people drawing imperceptibly closer, in an action both wondrous and knowing. As I dropped his hand for a moment to scratch my nose, then picked it up again, I thought about what it meant—especially what it meant to find holding someone's hand such a familiar action that you barely register how it feels anymore. It was a touch of hand on hand that spoke of memory and humor. A respect for the calluses on the tips of his fingers, and the slight raw-ness, a trademark of the regulation handwashing that marks his days. It was a touch that remembered. A mutual recall of the time when we had shared that moment, that moment of first starting out, the moment before you're really married, before you've fucked it up, or completely disappointed each other. Before you've really known what you were getting yourself into. A tactile recognition that we were still hold-ing hands despite it all. A renewed understanding that comes from the recognition of tetchiness, of seeing miscarriage and childbirth. Of driving down the M4 while one half of the marriage removes the hair from her upper lip with a small metal torture device and the other negotiates a tailback. Of arguments about money and time and failures of tact. Of racing to the hospital to find his father in cardiac arrest, and standing there, watching helplessly, the doctors unable to resuscitate, while he was busy parking the car. Of knowing someone so well you know that when he scratches his thumb in his palm, he's trying not to cry. But also, somehow, of not knowing him at all.

Real marriage, the one that came with the white dress and the bridesmaids and the vicar, is a peculiar mirage. Marriage is not an event, but a process. It is an unfolding and refolding of two selves in time, and with all the ordinariness that time brings.

After marriage, we must have what Stanley Cavell calls the comedy of remarriage. By this, he means something other than a wedding blessing and eternity rings. More of a realization. An accommodation—much like one might accommodate oneself to a too-small seat in the back of a car, squeezed in between two children's car seats and a pile of bags, as your knees are bent up to your chin and someone is being sick. A becoming accustomed to scenes of breastfeeding a child in the backseat by kneeling backward and hanging your boob into her mouth while she is still strapped into her child seat when there's no lay-by and she won't stop screaming. A screwball comedy of errors, which recognizes the fact that we do not go to bed in satin nor wake up in a good mood. It's not a million miles away from what Tolstoy writes about too. What mattered was what he called the family idea. For him, the entire movement of a novel was away from what we might understand as romance. For Tolstoy, in a marriage, love remains, but it is not the old love that one began with. Sofia writes about this too. Something in marriage has changed. It is always changing.

Hollywood of the 1940s loved this idea. *It Happened One Night*, *Bringing Up Baby*, *The Philadelphia Story*, *My Favorite Wife*. They look like capers on the surface. People get drunk

and chase leopards, or turn up in their pajamas and accidentally commit bigamy, but underneath the surface are stories
of couples in which lives shatter into fragments, in order to
be rearranged in different shapes. In these films, the point
of the story is *not* to get down the aisle. The films want, says
Cavell, *not to get the central pair together, but to get them* back
*together, together* again . . . *Only those can genuinely marry who
are already married. It is as though you know you are married
when you come to see that you cannot divorce, that is, when you
find your lives simply will not disentangle. If your love is lucky,
this knowledge will be greeted with laughter.*

The sermon in the church that day was a harsh one, and it
seemed to have no natural shape or possible end. I fiddled
with the clasp of my bag as I waited for my husband to write
back. The flames would be just licking around the bedroom
door by now, smoke beginning to build up a head of pressure at the front window. I wondered how long it would take
for the fire to reach the ground floor. It was our fourth wedding that year, and the vicar had decided to dispense with
the usual niceties about understanding and fallibility, and go
for a full-on campaign in which marriage was compared to a
battlefield, demanding courage, stoicism, and a pith helmet.
Marriage, he said, was like Afghanistan. A wave of suppressed
laughter made its way round the congregation. A baby started
to cry, and its sibling began to run into the vestry, hammer-
ing at the door. The organ creaked into action for the third
hymn. "All Things Bright and Beautiful."

Underneath my question are six words, written in his
careful hand.

*It's probably OK.*

Then a space. A pause. I remember watching as he wrote it.

*I love you.*

# BANBURY
## —2016—

PEOPLE WHEEL UP TO THE DOORS AT BANBURY STATION, dragging their suitcases by the handles, or stepping onto the train holding bags of crisps. The sounds are mechanical. The graceful cyborg announces the station stops as we get close, never quickening or slowing, never irritated. The triple beeps of opening doors and sighs of train carriages as they grind to a halt. It is not a recording but a real guard who blows a whistle, three short blasts, then one, a human grace note within the machine that we hear but do not see. We glide off past the dark mirror-clad car park, and the next station stop in the service will be Oxford. The refreshment bar at the front of the car is still open, and I look out at the fields of yellow and green, cut across by the dual carriageway. Two men now sit opposite me, both staring at their tablets. A banana lies on the table between them. I see the steeple of a church I cannot place, the tracks of the railway and a pile of pallets stacked high to my left. Then a cluster of cows and horses, and hay bales wrapped in black polythene like enormous rolls of liver pâté. A viaduct, and the flash of caravan parks and barges— and the flicker of green and yellow green and yellow. I am speeding faster and faster through a landscape that I know is near to home, but which I still don't recognize. I head down to use the loo, but it's IN USE, and I give up waiting in the vestibule.

The difficulty of writing about a life is the innumerable risks you take with the lives of others. There are people in my version of the story (that's all it is, my version) who have only just made it in around the edges—and for that, perhaps, they are glad. These minor characters, whose lives may not be as minor to me as I have suggested. The problem with not writing about these others is the false centrality of self that it creates, the floodlight I have shone upon myself. They, too, should have a "case," as Henry James said. Their own bag. Their own *sac à vider, un sac, un cas*. If only for me to hide in.

My husband. It is so hard to write about my husband that I don't even know what to call him. If I were to ask him, he would probably suggest that I just use his name, an idea that would strike me with its pragmatism, and its honesty. Properties I seek. When will I dare to let him read these thoughts? My guess is that he knows most of them already, both the love and the pain, the distance. There is something in the writing of this, I know, that is both a way of holding us apart and pulling us together. In some ways, this story keeps me shut away safe in my fictional compartment, my memory carriage. This story is my double time, my door to a world that is mine alone, my way to self-possession. Like the glass cabinet of books, the story keeps me possessed. But I write it partly for him, too, risky though it may be. When I show him these words, my inner world, which depends entirely on its secrecy for its existence, will collapse into something shared. It will no longer belong to me. If I risk what I value, maybe that's because something else might offer more. An opening. You can only go so far living behind glass. My husband has, besides, probably seen and heard most of it before. Keeper of secrets, he sits all day behind a desk while patients tell him what they would never dare tell another soul. The Hippocratic oath, like the seal of the confessional. He probably thinks this way himself. Don't we all? There is nothing as banal as our belief in our own originality. *That has been said before.*

And then, of course, there's you. You who are dying, in a room I will never see, in a place I would never recognize, except by virtual glimpses. *Dying, Egypt, dying*, as you'd have said to me, with a smile and a wave. All I can do now is imagine, but that is not nothing.

I never went to see you, that night after the exhibition, when I imagined you might have written to me. I had the deception and the outfit ready. I was, in my mind, so nearly there. But the sound of my baby daughter in the back of the car brought me back. It was pitch black. I flicked on the car lights, my heart beating fast. She gurgled happily, and laughed, and I felt the tears of self-reproach prick my eyes. Anna Karenina believed in omens—there was mine. A signal on the line, which brought me back from that road of double lives.

And I cannot go now. Now is not my time to be with you, and then wasn't either. It was impossible, as you would say. Impossible. We have missed each other's trains. Our time-tables did not match up. It's quite possible we wouldn't have liked traveling together after all. But as I write this, I think there is no harm in saying that I still think of you and your train. I think there is no harm in saying that I hope this book lands on your desk before you die. I hope you can see something in this. A glimpse of a face you can recognize. I hope you know that it was far more than nearly.

# OXFORD

## —2016—

I KEEP MY OWN COMPARTMENTS. THERE'S SOMETHING sealed about my world. There is home, and there is work, divided by a transparent wall. I make my way from one to the other by foot or bicycle, carrying bags of paper. I keep my books at work, apart from the few I need at home. The home books are stored in a glass-fronted cupboard, as if to keep them in place, securely bound. The worlds must not collide. If they did, I fear that one or the other might, perhaps, transform. Combust, change its state, oxidize, disappear into thin air. I keep no photographs of my family in my office. I take none of my home mess there, but make a separate work mess. My work world is through that door, divided, separate, apart. Sometimes I wonder why I avoid bringing my handbag into the room where I lecture—why I hide it behind a chair when I teach. When I teach I want to be a person with no baggage. It is this fiction of completeness which allows me to listen to the stories of others.

And that world is full of people with compartments of their own, their own glass walls. It is full of my students, who come to see me every day, with essays and plans and the odd crisis. We are on different trains, and this is as it should be. Their lives and mine never quite meet, but brush against each other at speed, registering each other the way trains pass, rocking momentarily on their tracks with the speed of the encounter. And then they leave.

Last month I watched fifty such leavers walk into a hall

to take their final examinations. They were a varied group, brought together by the task of getting a degree, and they brought little else with them. A pile of messenger bags and rucksacks, abandoned to comply with the regulations, sat outside the door, underneath the screens directing them to the correct examination room. I had set the paper. I looked down the lines as they checked the desks, figuring out where they should sit, then up at the portraits, which looked down on them in turn. Lines of ghosts. Most of the living looked deep in thought, but some exchanged a smile. A few carried a bottle of water. Some clutched a single Biro. Most held a small clear bag, gathered like a delicate bladder. There was something sad and heroic about these see-through bags, with their tissues, pencils, and Polo mints covered in fuzz. One by one, they took their seats at the fold-out desks and bent their heads as if in prayer. The bags, disgorging their contents onto each desk, spoke of a moment where there was nowhere to hide, and little to hold on to.

Sixty years ago, sophomores sitting down to take an exam at Cornell University might have felt similarly exposed. As they turned over the paper, they prepared to write about the European novel. Expecting topics about religion and social class, the questions instead asked them to describe Emma Bovary's sunshade and shoes, map the Liffey's movement through James Joyce's Dublin, and enumerate the contents of Anna Karenina's handbag. This unusual exam about unusually great novels was set by one of the world's greatest novelists and if the questions seem almost idle or frivolous, Nabokov certainly didn't intend them to be seen that way. In reading, one should notice and fondle the details. *Detail*, Nabokov told his students, *is everything*.

The red handbag must have been left lying on the railway line, a few feet away from Anna's body, near the edge of the platform. Nobody would have picked it up for hours, I suppose. The station master would have been the first to run down the platform, in his absurd multicolored hat. A crowd would have followed him, shouting, running back again, asking questions, half-horrified, half-fascinated by the scene. All their attention would have been on her body, on an attempt to revive a woman who had been crushed by the weight of Russian iron. People would have gathered round, asking if anyone recognized her. Her coachman would have made his way to the front of the crowd, barely believing his mistress could have done such a thing.

To a traveler, waiting on the other side of the platform, Anna's handbag would have stood out. Bright red—almost tomato-colored—the soft, vulnerable silk still shining on the ground. It would be gathered together by a cord, slightly worn from her travels, the end of one tassel beginning to fray. Someone surely would have rescued the bag as it lay there on the ground, a little apart from its owner. I hope they would. There's a risk, of course, that an opportunist might have filched it in the flurry. But I think that before too long, one of the station guards, or a policeman, would have brought it in—and handed it to her driver, who would have held it with a mixture of reverence and awkwardness as he telegraphed to Vronsky and awaited an answer. He would have looked at the clock as he sat there, watching the hands move slowly, and feeling the things in her bag, underneath the silk, the remnants of a self.

What, then, is in Anna's handbag? What sundry items spill out onto the railway tracks at Obiralovka Station on that day in May 1876? Perhaps these:

1. Cambric handkerchiefs
2. A photo album
3. A paper knife
4. A cushion
5. Some opium (she drinks her usual dose before she leaves the house)
6. Some form of contraceptive—maybe a sheath for Vronsky, but probably the newly invented Dutch cap (a diaphragm)
7. An imaginary novel by Anthony Trollope

But most important of all, perhaps, is a book. Not the novel by Trollope that we saw Anna reading on the train—but a book of her own making. A book that she would have written on her lap as she traveled, collating the manuscript pages as she worried about her lover, wrote letters to her husband, and packed and unpacked her bag. This book is one detail of *Anna Karenina* that rarely gets a mention. It is, admittedly, one of the many hundreds of items that clutter and cluster in the pages. It lives alongside the mushrooms and the hand-kerchiefs and the absence of milk and the death of a cow. A detail.

Near the novel's end, Stepan speaks of his sister's loneliness to a family friend as they sit together, jolting in a carriage. Anna's friends and family have started to notice it. She seems bereft, almost deadened by her situation. She is desperate for company. The friend wonders why Anna would be lonely: she has a child, a new baby daughter, as well as her son, as consolation. Stepan, in an unprecedented moment of enlightenment, corrects him. Women, he points out, are not simply breeder hens, or incubators. They are not simply bags for carrying others. Anna, he explains, assuages her loneliness by writing. She is writing, we learn, *a children's book and does not speak of it to anyone.* She is looking for a publisher. Anna is a parent *and* a writer. How to be both?

In 1999, a woman walked into the Oxford Examination Schools to sit her English finals, treading the same path through the desks as the students I watched last month. Her name was Kate Gross. (Another Kate.) She would have sat the five papers over five days. Five days of Chaucer and Shakespeare and Behn and Milton. I went to the library and called up the bound copies of the question papers she took that May. Imagined her looking through the questions, chewing the top of her Biro.

All disguise in Shakespeare is benevolent.

Contempt for women remains a major theme.

Is Skelton a transitional writer?

All reproduction is interpretation.

There is nothing outside the text.

Discuss.

Kate Gross was a brave person, and a traveler, like Kate Field. She traveled to Africa. She was private secretary to two prime ministers. She was destined to shine brightly, and briefly. She died at thirty-six, of bowel cancer. Her children, like Anna's, were still small. She had twin boys. Gross wrote a book about life and death, *Late Fragments.* I read it one afternoon, through the night and into the next morning, and I cried again and again about the loss of a parent. I cried for myself and the child that I was. What struck me, in the bravery of that book, as Kate looked into the light and dark of death, was her honesty about the power that writing gave her. When asked why she would spend her precious final weeks writing, rather than with her children, she was candid about the way that writing was an affirmation of selfhood, a way of holding herself together, and a way of remembering the person that she used to be.

Her book's epigraph says something more. *There are two copies of this book that matter*, she says on its opening page.

> There are two pairs of eyes I imagine reading every word. There are two adult hands which I hope will hold a battered paperback when others have long forgotten me and what I have to say.

Kate's book, then, is a children's book.

Perhaps not conventionally so. But it is written to be something for her children to read, to treasure, to hold, when she can hold them no longer. I think of my children's small hands.

Writing is better than nothing. Better than thin air.

We are closer to my home now, and nobody near me is reading. The carriage has emptied out and the seats nearby bear the familiar detritus of a journey. An empty water bottle and a container of sandwiches are abandoned on the flip-down table across the aisle, and part of a free newspaper has fallen to the floor. Out of the window I see the flocks of sheep, the poplar trees and hedges and hedgerows. A lorry goes by, bearing the legend *Enjoy Lunch!* Someone has thrown a small plastic doll down the side of the railway bank. She lies naked, upside down, legs open, with only a plastic bottle for company. Then a sea of innumerable retail chains, and on to the banks of tree branches, the horses wearing coats, the warehouse for Travis Perkins—a thousand shades of green, pushing their way through the boundaries of the netball court, reckless and refusing.

It matters that it is a children's book that Tolstoy imagines Anna writing. This is a gripping detail, one to hold on to. It is something that is irrefutably central to Anna, a woman who lost both her parents as a child. She is depressed, angry, and lonely. And she is writing a children's book. It is a book that we in turn might imagine, sitting in its battered cover on her son's bedside table—or that her plump, rosy little girl will one day read and wonder at as she grows older. Seryozha is nine when Anna dies. Her daughter, a little Anna, is still a baby. By the turn of the twentieth century, the boy with the frowning eyes and laughing smile would be a man.

In the act of writing a book, Anna is holding her children at arm's length. It's something that she does. Pulling them close, then pushing them away. Sitting on trains, looking at photographs of them in her album, set in time. She cannot bear to stay in the nursery for long. Something about her children, especially Annie, the mirror of herself, makes her afraid. The writing, perhaps, is a kind of compulsion, a kind of excuse.

Being a mother and a writer is not the easiest of logistical exercises. Being a writer makes mothering more difficult. Sometimes it's impractical. Or near impossible. *Here's the catch*, writes Maggie Nelson. *I cannot hold my baby at the same time as I write.* Catching and throwing. Holding and dropping. When I only had one child, and he was small, I could type with one hand, while I held him in my other arm and fed him. It was slow, but it gave me time to think. And the feeding gave me an excuse to sit still. That only lasted as long as he stayed still. With two children, I waited until he slept in a buggy in the hall and then typed standing up, with my daughter strapped vertically to me in a sling. That gave me about an hour a day, maximum, and if someone rang the doorbell, it was over. If the carefully titrated combination of sleep patterns went awry, there was no time at all. And often, simply getting them to that point left me too wrung out to write. Now they are rarely silent, and they see the time I spend staring at a screen as time stolen from them. Why should they not? They lean over my shoulder, or type sentences into my work. If I write by hand, they join me, then begin to doodle on my paper. I understand their frustration. My attention is elsewhere. My gaze is somewhere over their left shoulder. And besides, they are hungry. I cannot write and cook fish fingers at the same time.

Children are those others who haunt the pages of this book. The children we might have had, or the ones we have never had. The imaginary children who would have been born, if passing flames had become lovers. They are half alive. Dwellers in Hilary Mantel's *sly state of half becoming*. The *shadowland of chances missed*.

And the children we once were. Children who have had to grow up too soon, but in growing, leave a ghost child behind. I have one of those. My small blonde familiar, lost somewhere in a Finchley garden, wearing a green dress with yellow flowers. I have photos of her, with smiling eyes, before the frown set in. The young Kate Field had a child self too, treading the boards with her father. Anna's children, and the child that Anna was once. These ghost children are met with everywhere, these nearly beings. Some of us are quicker to see them than others, but they spook us all, waiting at those stations we pass by at speed, while the direct line presses on. Those children in the apple tree, *Not known, because not looked for / But heard, half heard, in the stillness.*

It feels, to me, as if there is never enough of myself that I can give to my children. Even if I were to hold nothing back, they would be left wanting. In their wholeness and their present loveliness, they deserve so much more than the fragmentary bits that I staple together, daily, into a person. I do not feel this always. This is just one of the stories that comes from one of my distracted array of selves, the draft versions of me. But it emerges from time to time. It's hard to explain quite what loss takes away from a heart. If you were to dissect me, I feel as if one particular organ might look depleted and dented, still with the essence of itself, but not quite as it should be.

Given this, I wonder why I take so much time away from them. Why should I take time to look out of train windows, to type on a keyboard, to think of the ways in which words might be placed against words. Sometimes I steal time from sleep. I wake at 5 a.m. and creep down the stairs. I make cups of bad instant coffee and write to the tune of the buzzing fridge at dawn. Or sit and watch the wall. Should I not, even in this stolen time, go back upstairs to be with them as they sleep? Time is passing, and they will not be like this for long.

The stilled photographs are an illusion, just like the illusion of my memory of them. Our son sleeps with his arms held back, a perfect profile, like one of Botticelli's cupids. He sleeps lightly, and wakes if you turn a light off. He dreams of falling down stairs, or of an octopus that lives in our kitchen. Our daughter is curled in a ball under a Disney princess duvet, her tow-colored hair hiding her beautiful baby face. So fast asleep that she can roll off the mattress and onto the floor without flinching.

I walk into the bathroom and see my face in the mirror, framed by a row of novelty toothbrushes. The fool. The screwball. To be a 1950s comedy wife, you have to learn to fool about. For what people do together is, as Cavell says, *less important than the fact that they do whatever it is together, that they know how to spend time together, even that they would rather waste time together than do anything else—except that no time they are together could be wasted.* Life is not the search for epiphanies. But how to write that down? How to write, *and* be together? How are we to live together?

I wonder if I will always be drawn to the myth of together, no matter how I run away. It is a myth that always puts the pair at the center. Whether it is the screwball couple or the Russian lovers, whether you end up with Crosby or Vronsky, the love triangle always ends in a line, a partnering of man and woman, hand in hand. It's an image I have been shown so many times. That banal commonplace that Doris Lessing says everyone knows. It is the one you hung on the wall.

If I seem to have trained my lens too much upon the triangle and the line, the man and the woman, it is because I cannot find a new shape until I examine the one that I have held for so long. It is also because the shape of this commonplace has been my truth. Not to tell it would be to cancel myself out.

I fear my exhibition is a broken version of yours. A parody. (Parody is a byway of tenderness. It is also power.) Time to frame myself.

Things are developing still. Slowly does it. Ever so gradually, in Sarony's Broadway studio, two faces appear. Layer by layer, two bodies come into focus. A man and a woman, his arm around her waist. He is older than she is, by some twenty years or so. Perhaps even thirty. They do not look as if they have done this before, but they both stare at the lens, almost boldly, as if challenging the viewer to stop them. See if we care, they seem to say. See. It took more than just a moment or two. Twenty seconds were counted, each figure looking into the dense glass circles of the lens, each for a moment living together. The chronology has printed itself onto the glass. Measured out in particles, chemicals changing states, changing properties. The younger man touches his teacher's hands as they pass the plate between them. By accident, perhaps. A hand slips on the edge, slides, the fluid moves. One false move. You cannot go back now. The plate shatters on the floor. Irrevocable past. Glass is everywhere.

Perhaps writing is itself an act of holding. As a life closes in on itself, nearing its end with each turn of the page, writing is a way of distilling, of warding off that moment. Writing is a not melting away into a sea of forgetting, a not fading away like an old photograph too long in the sun. It can be an act of discovery, too. Of remembering something that you never realized you had lost, or of discovering something that hasn't even happened yet, and grasping it. Writing can be more than finding, even. It can be winning. Writing is tactile. It's touching, even if what it offers is not quite the same kind of touch as the warmth of another's hand, or the powerful, dry heat of another body. The book has a different, touching kind of power. A different strength.

The book, after all, has the power to endure something. Something intimate. Something that—at the end of her life—Anna Karenina can no longer bear. She has run from everything. She has left her son. Her daughter, her baby. Her husband. Her lover. Nothing and nobody can hold her. But her book endures, and will endure beyond her. Assuming, of course, that someone finds the manuscript pages, lying there beside that railway line. Assuming someone picks them up and gathers them in. Her book—perhaps any book—is a way of being close to someone, while keeping your distance. It frames. It gives a certain light. The book can be held.

The train has pulled in now, though the engine is still running. The platform is shining wet under the strip lights. We come to rest on the exit side of the station, and by this time the barriers are all open, as well as the side gate into the car park. We are a little late, due to the delay after Banbury, but I am still in time. Only a little further behind than I expected. I can make it up. I can make it up. I've been doing that for some time.

Soon—not long now—I will get off the bus that stops near the chip shop and the mini roundabout. I'll walk down the road, past the house with the barking dog and the skip that never seems to go. The sound of trains is distant but still audible. I will round the corner and open the gate, which squeaks as I push it.

I've been a good way. They do not know that I have not been to see you, and that you are dying now. *The last word is not said*. Now is the time to let them in. I close the book. I will pick up my bag and go home.

# SOURCES OF QUOTATIONS

**DEPARTURES**

2    **a lovely day:** Bill Withers, vocalist, lyric from "Lovely Day (Sunshine Mix)," by Bill Withers and Skip Scarborough, produced by Bill Withers and Clarence McDonald, remixed by Ben Liebrand, Chelsea Music, CBS, 1988, vinyl.

**HULL TO FERRIBY**

5    *All happy families are alike . . .* : Leo Tolstoy, *Anna Karenina*, trans. Rosamund Bartlett (Oxford: Oxford University Press, 2014), 3.

**ST. PETERSBURG TO MOSCOW**

8    *muffled, hoarfrost-covered driver . . . puffing steam:* Leo Tolstoy, *Anna Karenina*, trans. Bartlett, 62.

10    *minute and infinitesimally small:* Leo Tolstoy, "Why Do Men Stupefy Themselves?," in *Essays and Letters*, trans. Aylmer Maude (London: Grant Richards, 1903), 28.

10    *watch keeps time . . . keeps pace with our pulses:* Vladimir Nabokov, *Lectures on Russian Literature* (New York: Harcourt Brace, 1981), 141.

10    *"Every heart has its own skeletons," as the English say:* Leo Tolstoy, *Anna Karenina*, trans. Constance Garnett (London: Heinemann, 1977), 100.

12    **Human error:** "Hull Hospital Remembers 1927 Train Crash Victims," *BBC News*, February 10, 2012, http://www.bbc.co.uk/news/uk-england -humber-16978180; see also J. W. Pringle to the Ministry of Transport, "Report on the Accident That Occurred at Hull Paragon on 14 February 1927," April 13, 1927, http://www.railwaysarchive.co.uk /docsummary.php?docID=308 and *Express Train Disaster* (1927), silent film footage, 1:50, https://www.youtube.com/watch?v=WBBzLjExbp0.

**FERRIBY TO BROUGH**

14    *No more sombre enemy of good art than the pram in the hall:* Cyril Connolly, *Enemies of Promise* (Chicago: University of Chicago Press, 2008), 116.

203

## ST. PETERSBURG TO MOSCOW

18  **reading English novels:** See Sofia Tolstoy, diary entry for October 23, 1878, *The Diaries of Sofia Tolstoy*, trans. Cathy Porter (Richmond: Alma Books, 2010), 53.

18  **the make-believe of a beginning:** "Men can do nothing without the make-believe of a beginning," George Eliot, *Daniel Deronda* (Oxford: Oxford University Press, 2014), 3.

## HACKNEY WICK

19  *Summer in the city*: Aztec Camera, "Somewhere in My Heart," by Roddy Frame, produced by Michael Jonzun, WEA, 1987, vinyl.

## BATTERY PLACE TO CORTLANDT STREET

20  **all life and expression:** "Photography in the Great Exhibition," *The Philadelphia Photographer*, 184–86, quoted in Erin Pauwels, "Resetting the Camera's Clock: Sarony, Muybridge & the Aesthetics of Wet-Plate Photography," *History and Technology* 31, no. 4 (October 2015): 484.

23  *The last word is not said*: Joseph Conrad, *Lord Jim* (Oxford: Oxford University Press, 2008), 163.

23  **sick at heart:** Kate Field, diary entry for January 1, 1869, quoted in Lilian Whiting, *Kate Field: A Record* (Boston: Little, Brown, 1899), 196.

23  **acrobatic, airy, and perched-up:** *New York Times*, January 12, 1868.

## BROUGH TO GOOLE

25  *full front . . . natural look*: Anthony Trollope to Kate Field, June 18, 1868, in *The Letters of Anthony Trollope*, ed. N. John Hall (Stanford, CA: Stanford University Press), 1: 433.

25  *Can anything indeed . . .* : Quoted in Whiting, *Kate Field*, 194.

27  *clock for seeing*: "cameras, in short, were clocks for seeing," Roland Barthes, *Camera Lucida: Reflections on Photography*, trans. Richard Howard (London: Vintage, 2000), 15.

27  *Please, sir, I want*: Charles Dickens, *Oliver Twist* (Harmondsworth, UK: Penguin, 1966), 56.

27  *I attribute the power of doing this altogether . . .* : Anthony Trollope, *An Autobiography and Other Writings*, ed. Nicholas Shrimpton (Oxford: Oxford University Press, 2014), 169.

27  *If you are going . . .* : Trollope to Field, June 3, 1868, *Letters*, 1: 432.

28  **edge of dread:** Adrienne Rich, "What Kinds of Times Are These," in *Collected Poems 1950–2012*, ed. Claudia Rankine (New York: Norton, 2016), 755.

## WEST FINCHLEY TO BELSIZE PARK

31   *can only be relieved . . .*: J. G. Ballard, quoted in Chris Hall, "Millennium People: Entertaining Violence," *Spike Magazine*, January 1, 2004, https://www.spikemagazine.com/0104jgballard.

37   *eternullity*: See Maurice Blanchot's review of Henri Lefebvre, "the everyday is our portion of eternity: the eternullity of which Laforgue speaks," in Maurice Blanchot, *The Infinite Conversation*, trans. Susan Hanson (Minneapolis: University of Minnesota Press, 1993), 245.

38   *I don't like mountains . . .*: Quoted in Richard Davenport-Hines, *Auden* (London: Minerva, 1995), 98.

39   *no possibility of taking a walk that day*: Charlotte Brontë, *Jane Eyre* (London: Penguin, 1996), 13.

## BAKER STREET TO MOORGATE STREET

46   *pasticcio of rain*: "Kate Field on London," *St. Louis Globe-Democrat*, November 8, 1885, 14.

48   **black fumes, . . . prayer meetings:** George Gissing, *In the Year of Jubilee* (CreateSpace, 2014), 146.

48   **small pear-shaped wooden instrument:** Kate Field, *The History of Bell's Telephone* (London: Bradbury, Agnew, 1878), 14–17, quoted in Gary Scharnhorst, *Kate Field: The Many Lives of a Nineteenth-Century American Journalist* (New York: Syracuse University Press, 2008), 126.

48   *every house will be connected*: Field, *History of Bell's Telephone*, quoted in Scharnhorst, *Kate Field*, 126.

48   **a large party of swells:** Kate Field to Edmund Clarence Stedman, March 14, 1878, in *Kate Field: Selected Letters*, ed. Carolyn J. Moss (Carbondale: Southern Illinois University Press, 1996), 141.

50   *If you like it I will take you . . .*: Trollope to Field, "Monday Morning," circa 1873–80, *Letters*, 2: 1000.

50   *If you'll go down close to the sea . . .*: Trollope to Field, July 8, 1868, *Letters*, 1: 437–38.

50   **black phantom:** Trollope to Field, July 13, 1868, *Letters*, 1: 439.

50   **enveloped in buffalo furs:** Anthony Trollope, "Miss Ophelia Gledd," in *Early Short Stories*, ed. John Sutherland (Oxford: Oxford University Press, 1994), 450.

50   **have liked to cross the Rocky Mountains . . . and the Pampas:** Trollope, 450.

51   **in the corner . . . waiting:** "Recollections by Kate Field," *New York Tribune*, December 24, 1880, quoted in Whiting, *Kate Field*, 397.

51   **one of the "taking" things of the season:** See the *Hartford Courant*, March 20, 1878, 1, quoted in Scharnhorst, *Kate Field*, 129.

## MOSCOW

56 My description of Brent Cross Shopping Centre is indebted to Nilu Zia's "40 Years of Brent Cross," *Vice*, March 7, 2016, https://www .vice.com/en_uk/article/mvkawb/love-letter-40-years-of-brent-cross. Accessed October 3, 2023.

57 **microcosm of our world and identity:** Kerry Potter, "What to Know When Buying a New Handbag," *The Pool*, February 21, 2017.

58 **a particular fear: of injury, of discomfort, of boredom, of attack:** Quoted in Robert Moor, *On Trails: An Exploration* (New York: Simon & Schuster, 2016), 325.

59 **Perhaps even her tears:** I owe this idea to the beautiful essay by Axelle Ropert, who writes of Mary Poppins's bag "*si ce sac généreux en démonstations colorées témoignait aussi de la pudeur de Mary, recelant toutes les larmes incolores qu'elle a voulu garder pour elle?*" [as if this multicolored bag of tricks also bore witness to Mary's shame, hiding within its depths those empty, colorless tears that she wished to keep within her, and for herself]. "12 films, 12 sacs. Une anthologie" in *Le Cas du Sac*, ed. Farid Chenoune (Paris: Hermès, 2004), 84.

60 **a womb veil:** Also known as the "Ladies' patent shield" or "The Wife's Protector," it was available in the late nineteenth century by mail order for about $6.

## GOOLE TO THORNE NORTH

All references on pages 63–67 are taken from advertisements that appeared in *The Times*, 1875:

**LOST, A CARRIAGE CLOCK:** January 4.

**lady's sealskin muff-bag:** January 7.

**nothing of value except papers, which are important only to the owner:** See, for example, the entries for December 15, June 19, October 14.

**a London dock warrant:** October 26.

**a cane of Brazilian palm:** January 16.

**a map of the British Channel:** November 25.

**an opal brooch:** May 18.

**a small case of surgical instruments:** August 4.

**BALLOON LOST . . . :** August 12.

**AMULET:** August 30.

**WILL a Black Swan . . . :** December 24.

**A young gentleman, age 26 . . . fair and pale complexion:** January 28, February 2, February 10, February 11, February 13.

**very depressed and emaciated appearance:** February 6.

**lost gold Albert chain:** January 4.

**If you have any regard for yourself:** January 4.

**A black bearskin carriage rug:** May 21.

LOST.—TWENTY POUNDS REWARD shall be given for a BROWN LEATHER CASE: January 7.

FRED D.L.—There will be a letter: January 15.

A.T.—If you return at once: January 15.

T. to W.—Meet me on Monday or Tuesday: January 16.

LOST, during the last fortnight: January 23.

black leather porte-monnaie purse: February 9.

MOTHER, Dear: February 6.

BLACK BAG RECEIVED: May 19.

MANUSCRIPT LENT: May 21.

hansom cab in Fleet Street: June 19.

LOST, on Tuesday, either in Chapel-street or Belgrave-square: June 17.

BLACK PORTMANTEAU LOST: August 14.

LOST, a GOLD LOCKET, heart-shaped: June 23.

gold locket.—LOST, from the Paddington Terminus: June 19.

E.P., who left Eastbourne by the 2 p.m.: August 14.

MISSING.—£10 REWARD.—LEFT SHEFFIELD: August 18.

MYSTERIOUSLY DISAPPEARED . . . : November 9.

THE ONE OF THE VALLEY—You do not know . . . : October 16.

Mrs. T: see, for examples, adverts placed on October 13, 1871; December 20, 1872; October 17, 1873; December 20, 1873.

W. writes that he wishes to see his friend at 96: January 26.

TO C.—Write to me . . . : May 19.

Have you forgotten me and the pretty gardens? . . . : October 12.

HENRY.—Your return will be most welcome: October 16.

BR.—Same address . . . : February 9.

## THORNE NORTH TO DONCASTER

72    *mess terrorist*: Eric Abrahamson and David H. Freedman, *A Perfect Mess: The Hidden Benefits of Disorder* (New York: Weidenfeld & Nicolson, 2014), 100.

## MOSCOW TO ST. PETERSBURG

79    *The railroad is to travel as a whore is to love*: Leo Tolstoy to Ivan Turgenev, 1857; see Moisei Altman, *Chitaia Tolstogo* (Tula: Priokskoe knizhnoe izdatel'stvo, 1966), 118, reprinted in Daniel Rancour-Laferriere, *Tolstoy on the Couch* (London: Macmillan, 1998), 59.

80    **good accustomed**: Leo Tolstoy, *Anna Karenina*, trans. Louise and Aylmer Maude (Ware, UK: Wordsworth, 1999), 98.

80    **loss of limbs, eyes, . . . or death**: *Railway Passengers Assurance Company, Instructions to Station Agents*, 1897, 29. I am grateful to Christopher Gray and David Turner for their help with this information, and to

Dr. Turner's blog entry on railway insurance at http://turniprail
.blogspot.com/2011/05/at-time-of-catastrophe-railway.html, where
this text is reprinted.

80 **vibrations:** See Charles Malchow, *The Sexual Life: Embracing the
Natural Sexual Impulse* (St Louis: C. V. Mosby, 1915), 57.


**SHEFFIELD TO BIRMINGHAM NEW STREET**

85 **forcing-house:** E. M. Forster, *Howards End* (London: Random House,
1999), 191.

86 **the secret of reading . . . acting like carriage springs to the volume:**
George Measom, "Introduction," *The Official Illustrated Guide to the
South-Eastern Railway, and Its Branches* (London: Lowe and Brydon,
1858).


**BOLOGOYE STATION**

88 *Am I myself or someone else?*: Leo Tolstoy, *Anna Karenina*, trans.
Joel Carmichael (New York: Bantam, 2006), 120.

88 *tearing and whistling around the corner . . .* : Leo Tolstoy, *Anna Karenina*, trans. Bartlett, 102.

89 *their steps crackling . . .* : Leo Tolstoy, *Anna Karenina*, trans.
Garnett, 105.

90 *quivering light flashing in her eyes . . .* : Leo Tolstoy, *Anna Karenina*,
trans. Maude, 79.

90 *A feeling that both frightened her and made her happy*: Leo Tolstoy,
*Anna Karenina*, trans. Maude, 101–2.

90 **shame, joy, and horror:** Leo Tolstoy, *Anna Karenina*, trans. Maude,
147.

90 *describe all the complexity of those feelings . . .* : Leo Tolstoy,
*Anna Karenina*, trans. Maude, 147.

90 *No single word in English . . .* : Aleksandr Pushkin, *Eugene Onegin:
A Novel in Verse*, trans. with a commentary by Vladimir Nabokov
(London: Routledge & Kegan Paul, 1964), 2:141.

91 **shrined in double retirement:** Charlotte Brontë, *Jane Eyre* (London:
Penguin, 1985), 39.

91 *You are inside it; it is inside you . . .* : Georges Poulet, "The Phenome-
nology of Reading," *New Literary History* 1, no. 1 (October 1969): 54.

92 *a vast dying sea . . . jar of honey*: Nicholson Baker, *U & I* (London:
Granta, 1991), 32.

92 *dreaming lettuce in the garden*: W. G. Sebald, *Austerlitz* (London:
Penguin, 2011), 134.

## GHOST TRAIN

95   *None will do . . .* : Leo Tolstoy, diary entry for March 10, 1906, in
     Tolstoy's *Complete Collected Works*, Jubilee edition (1928–58), 55: 374.

95   **most observed of all observers:** Whiting, *Kate Field*, 54.

95   **The only one she adored:** See Field, diary entry, August 24, 1857, "He
     was the only one whom I adored," quoted in Whiting, Kate Field, 66.

96   *so sad, so strange, . . .* : See Whiting, *Kate Field*, 75, 59.

97   *Your Father:* Kate Field, *Planchette's Diary* (New York: Redfield Press,
     1868), 11.

98   *They were all dying . . .* : Trollope, *Autobiography*, 28.

98   *as he had lived . . .* : Anthony Trollope, *Barchester Towers* (London:
     J. M. Dent, 1931), 5, 7.

98   *He dared to ask himself . . .* : Trollope, *Barchester Towers*, 7.

99   *fleetness of time . . .* : Field, diary entry for January 1, 1869, quoted in
     Whiting, *Kate Field*, 196.

99   *losing a parent . . .* : Malcolm Gladwell, *David and Goliath: Underdogs,
     Misfits, and the Art of Battling Giants* (London: Penguin, 2014), 86.

## FINCHLEY CENTRAL TO BURNT OAK

105  *a cascade of secondary losses . . .* : adapted from Kathryn H. Howell
     et al., "Children Facing Parental Cancer v. Parental Death," *JCFS* 25
     (2016): 153.

106  *depression, criminal or disruptive behaviors, . . .* : Al Aynsley-Green
     et al., "Bereavement in Childhood: Risks, Consequences and
     Responses," *BMJ Supportive and Palliative Care* 2, no 1 (March 2012):
     2, https://spcare.bmj.com/content/bmjspcare/2/1/2.full.pdf

109  **not-to-die-of-ignorance:** See TBWA's public information film
     *AIDS: Don't Die of Ignorance* (1987).

## CHALK FARM TO BELSIZE PARK

111  *suck out all the marrow of life:* See Henry David Thoreau as quoted by
     Neil Perry in the film *Dead Poets Society* (1989).

111  **Losing farther, losing faster:** Elizabeth Bishop, "One Art," in *Complete
     Poems* (London: Chatto & Windus, 1991), 178.

112  *an athlete of the clock . . .* : John Updike, *Marry Me* (London: Penguin,
     2008), 2. I was reminded of this passage from Updike, and alerted
     to its significance in relation to time and death, by Katie Roiphe's
     chapter on John Updike in her brilliant *The Violet Hour: Great Writers
     at the End* (London: Virago, 2016). My discussion in this paragraph is
     indebted to her thinking.

112  *the devouring gray sensation of time:* John Updike, *Toward the End of
     Time* (New York: Alfred A. Knopf, 1997), 85.

116  *The art of losing:* Elizabeth Bishop, "One Art," 178.

## BIRMINGHAM NEW STREET TO LEAMINGTON SPA

123   *nursing, eating, drinking* . . . : Sofia Tolstoy, February 25, 1865, in Porter, *Diaries*, 24.

123   *I wish something would happen soon*: Sofia Tolstoy, November 3, 1864, in Porter, *Diaries*, 23.

124   *There is no such thing as love* . . . : Sofia Tolstoy, December 14, 1890, in Porter, *Diaries*, 79.

124   *I am . . . a piece of household furniture*: Sofia Tolstoy, November 13, 1863, in Porter, *Diaries*, 20.

124   *idiorhythmic*: See Roland Barthes, *How to Live Together: Novelistic Simulations of Some Everyday Spaces* (New York: Columbia University Press, 2002), 6 and passim.

## ELEPHANT AND CASTLE

129   **getting away with it**: Electronic, "Getting Away with It," *Electronic*, by Johnny Marr, Bernard Sumner, and Neil Tennant, produced by Bernard Sumner, Johnny Marr, and Neil Tennant, Factory, 1991, vinyl. (Released as a single in 1989.)

## EUSTON TO INVERNESS

142   **delicious dream**: Adapted from Lydia Child, *The Frugal Housewife: Dedicated to Those Who Are Not Ashamed of Economy* (London: T. T. and J. Tegg, 1832), 124.

143   **falling in love**: Leo Tolstoy, "Family Happiness," in *The Kreutzer Sonata and Other Stories* (Oxford: Oxford University Press, 2009), 150.

143   *difficult to imagine . . . Miss Field's presence and delivery*: *New York Times*, November 15, 1874.

144   *neither young nor handsome*: Quoted in Scharnhorst, *Kate Field*, 108.

144   **racetrack but a sort of Peacock Alley**: John Malcolm Brinnin, *The Sway of the Grand Saloon: A Social History of the North Atlantic* (London: Macmillan, 1971), 240.

144   *protesting stomachs . . . are systematically outraged*: Kate Field, "At Sea," in *Hap-Hazard* (Cambridge, MA: Welch, Bigelow, 1873), 94.

145   *excessively pretty—intelligent and piquante* . . . : *Globe* review, rep. in letter from Field to Stedman, May 1, 1876, *Selected Letters*, 123, 122.

146   *Very delightful. Very difficult*: Leo Tolstoy, *Anna Karenina*, trans. Maude, 476.

146   *the real satisfactions of a woman's life*: Field, diary entry for January 20, 1869, quoted in Whiting, *Kate Field*, 204.

146   *I am misunderstood*: Field, diary entry for January 18, 1869, quoted in Whiting, *Kate Field*, 204.

## CARNFORTH

160 ***at her own pace, . . . dragged along*:** Barthes, *How to Live Together*, 9.
163 ***there will be dying*:** Derek Mahon, "Everything Is Going to Be All Right," in *Collected Poems* (Oldcastle: Gallery Press, 1999), 38.

## TENWAY JUNCTION

165 ***Her little red handbag . . .* :** Leo Tolstoy, *Anna Karenina*, trans. Maude, 757.
165 ***Where am I? . . .* :** Leo Tolstoy, *Anna Karenina*, trans. Bartlett, 771.

## GRAND CENTRAL TO UTAH

168 **kindly; inimitable:** "Anthony Trollope," *The Times*, December 7, 1882, 6.
168 ***My marriage . . .* :** Trollope, *Autobiography*, 50.
170 ***It's time*:** Leo Tolstoy, *Anna Karenina*, trans. Bartlett, 114.
172 ***loving husband, a loving father, and a true friend*:** See Victoria Glendinning, *Trollope* (London: Hutchinson, 1992), 501.
172 **the nature of a fit:** *New York Times*, November 6, 1882.
172 **except that the power of speech:** *The Times*, November 14, 1882.
173 **losing his strength:** *The Times*, December 2, 1882.
173 **critical:** *The Times*, December 5, 1882.
173 ***an author at once so comfortable and so pleasant*:** *New York Times*, December 7, 1882.
173 **She only desired to be herself:** "I only desire to be myself," Kate Field in the *Boston Traveller*, September 28, 1882, quoted in Scharnhorst, *Kate Field*, 249.
174 ***I was adored once, too*:** Shakespeare, *Twelfth Night*, 2.3.175. All references to Shakespeare are taken from *The Complete Works*, edited by Stanley Wells and Gary Taylor (Oxford: Clarendon Press, 1986). References are to act, scene, and line of this edition.
175 ***Trollope kills me . . .* :** N. N. Glisev, *Chronicle of the Life and Work of L. N. Tolstoy* (Moscow, 1928), 315.
175 **American woman:** Trollope, *Autobiography*, 195.
175 ***She is a ray of light to me . . .* :** Trollope, 195.
176 ***Mormon monster*:** See Whiting, *Kate Field*, 448.
177 ***Don't talk to me about the equality of the sexes . . .* :** Kate Field, *Kate Field's Washington*, vol. 11, no. 11, March 16, 1895.
177 ***which is not the involuntary result of fleeting emotion . . .* :** W. H. Auden, *A Certain World: A Commonplace Book*, reprinted in *Prose 1969–1973*, ed. Edward Mendelson (Princeton, NJ: Princeton University Press, 2015), 6: 189.
177 ***I have stood all alone . . .* :** Kate Field to Whitelaw Reid, Dec 3, 1870, in *Selected Letters*, 65.

178   *Kodak-distant*: Philip Larkin, "Whatever Happened?," *Collected Poems*,
      ed. Anthony Thwaite (London: Faber & Faber, 1988), 74.
178   *All happy families resemble one another* . . . : Leo Tolstoy, *Anna Karen-
      ina*, trans. Nathan Dole (New York: Thomas J. Cromwell, 1886), 1.


## LEAMINGTON TO BANBURY

179   *By digging into our souls* . . . : Leo Tolstoy, *Anna Karenina*, trans.
      Maude, 144.
180   **a loaded gun:** Stacy Schiff, *Véra: Mrs. Vladimir Nabokov: A Biography*
      (London: Random House, 1999), 197.
180   *consenting not to be a single being*: Mollie Rose Quinn, "Interview
      with Maggie Nelson," *Atlas Review*, 4. I am indebted to Nelson's
      brilliant discussion of the categories of personal and public in this
      interview. As she writes, "Honestly words like personal, private,
      intimate, don't have an enormous amount of meaning to me right
      now . . . I'm into the complexities of the traffic between the individual
      and the group, into thinking about what Fred Moten means when
      he, after Glissant, talks about 'consenting not to be a single being.'
      This conversation is far more intriguing and urgent to me than any
      rehashing of the binary of the private and the public (a conversation
      in which women and people of color and transgender folk and so
      on don't usually fare very well, as their bodies tend to disrupt/be
      excluded from a particular conceptualization of the 'public,' so the
      dice are loaded before the roll)."
183   **family idea:** See Sofia Tolstoy, in her diary, quoting Leo Tolstoy,
      "For a work to be good, one has to love in it the main, fundamental
      idea. And so, in *Anna Karenina*, I love the family idea," March 3, 1877,
      quoted in Liza Knapp, *Anna Karenina and Others* (Madison: University
      of Wisconsin Press, 2016), 249; Leo Tolstoy, "Family Happiness," in
      *The Kreutzer Sonata and Other Stories*, 83.
184   *not to get the central pair together* . . . : Stanley Cavell, *Pursuits of
      Happiness: The Hollywood Comedy of Remarriage* (Cambridge, MA:
      Harvard University Press 1981), 2, 127.


## BANBURY

187   **have a "case":** Henry James, preface to *Wings of the Dove* (London:
      Penguin, 2008), 7.
187   **risk what I value:** See Jeanette Winterson, *The Guardian*, October 2,
      2001, https://www.theguardian.com/world/2001/oct/02/gender.uk1.
188   *That has been said before*: The previous sentence paraphrases W. H.
      Auden's statement that the "absolutely banal [is] my sense of my own
      uniqueness," *The Dyer's Hand* (New York: Vintage, 1989), 95.
188   *Dying, Egypt, dying*: Shakespeare, *Antony and Cleopatra*, 4.16.43.

**OXFORD**

190   describe Emma Bovary's sunshade . . . the contents of Anna Karenina's
      handbag: Vladimir Nabokov, *Lectures on Literature* (London: Mariner,
      1982), 385, and the Nabokov archive at Cornell—I am grateful to L. De
      La Durantaye's article "Kafka's Reality and Nabokov's Fantasy" (*Com-
      parative Literature* 59, no. 4: 318), for guiding me to this.

190   one should notice and fondle: Vladimir Nabokov, *Lectures on Litera-
      ture*, I.

190   *Detail is everything*: Vladimir Nabokov, *Strong Opinions* (New York:
      Vintage International, 1990), 168.

193   she has a child: Leo Tolstoy, *Anna Karenina*, trans. Maude, 685.

193   *a children's book and does not speak of it to anyone*: Leo Tolstoy, 685.

193   All disguise in Shakespeare is benevolent . . . Discuss: *Honour School
      of English Language and Literature 1999–2001*. Oxford: University of
      Oxford, 1987.

194   *There are two copies of this book that matter . . .* : Kate Gross, *Late
      Fragments: Everything I Want to Tell You (About this Magnificent Life)*
      (London: William Collins, 2015), front matter.

195   *Here's the catch . . .* : Maggie Nelson, *The Argonauts* (London: Melville
      House, 2016), 45.

196   *sly state of half becoming . . . shadowland of chances missed*: Hilary
      Mantel, *Giving Up the Ghost: A Memoir* (London: 4th Estate, 2010), 229.

197   *Not known, because not looked for . . .* : T. S. Eliot, *Little Gidding* in
      *Four Quartets* (London: Faber & Faber, 1950), 44.

198   *less important than the fact that they do whatever it is together . . .* :
      Cavell, *Pursuits of Happiness*, 88.

198   banal commonplace . . . that everyone knows: Doris Lessing, *The
      Golden Notebook* (London: 4th Estate, 2013), 283.

199   cancel myself out: Lessing, 283.

199   byway of tenderness: Gérard Genette, *Palimpsests: Literature in the
      Second Degree* (Lincoln: University of Nebraska Press, 1997), 120.

201   *The last word is not said*: Conrad, *Lord Jim*, 163.

# FURTHER READING
# AND SOURCES

## ON SOFIA TOLSTOY

*The Diaries of Sofia Tolstoy*. Foreword by Doris Lessing. Translated by Cathy
Porter. Richmond: Alma Books, 2010.

Bartlett, Rosamund, and Anna Benn. *Literary Russia: A Guide*. London:
Gerald Duckworth, 2007.

Bendavid-Val, Leah. *Song without Words: The Photographs & Diaries of
Countess Sophia Tolstoy*. New York: National Geographic Society,
2007.

## ON LEO TOLSTOY

*Catalogue of L. N. Tolstoy's Library in Iasnaia Poliana*. Vol. 3, edited by N. V.
Kotrelev. Tula, Russia: Iasnaia Poliana, 1999.

Bartlett, Rosamund. *Tolstoy: A Russian Life*. London: Profile, 2010.

Cruise, Edwina. "Tracking the English Novel in *Anna Karenina*: Who Wrote
the English Novel That Anna Reads?" In *Anniversary Essays on Tolstoy*,
edited by Donna Orwin, 159–82. Cambridge: Cambridge University
Press, 2010.

Gareth Jones, W. *Tolstoi and Britain*. Oxford: Berg, 1995.

Goubert, Denis. "Did Tolstoy Read *East Lynne*?" *Slavonic and East European
Review* 58, no. 1 (1980): 22–39.

Knapp, Liza. *Anna Karenina and Others*. Madison: University of Wisconsin
Press, 2016.

Mandelker, Amy. *Framing Anna Karenina: Tolstoy, the Woman Question, and
the Victorian Novel*. Columbus: Ohio State University Press, 1994.

Morson, Gary Saul. *Anna Karenina in Our Time: Seeing More Wisely*. New
Haven, CT: Yale University Press, 2007.

Nabokov, Vladimir. *Lectures on Russian Literature*. New York: Harcourt
Brace, 1981.

Parini, Jay. *The Last Station: A Novel of Tolstoy's Final Year*. London: Canongate Books, 2007.

Rancour-Laferriere, Daniel. *Tolstoy on the Couch: Misogyny, Masochism, and
the Absent Mother*. London: Macmillan, 1998.

Simmons, Ernest J. *Leo Tolstoy*. London: John Lehmann, 1949.

Stenbock-Fermor, Elisabeth. *The Architecture of Anna Karenina*. Lisse, Neth-
erlands: Peter de Ridder Press, 1975.

Sutherland, John. "What English Novel Is Anna Karenina Reading?" In *Who Betrays Elizabeth Bennet?*, 219–23. Oxford: Oxford University Press, 1999.

Tolstoy, Leo. *Anna Karenina*. Translated by Rosamund Bartlett. Oxford: Oxford University Press, 2016.

Tolstoy, Leo. *Anna Karenina*. Translated by Nathan Dole. New York, 1886. This is the edition that Kate Field would have read.

Tolstoy, Leo. *Anna Karenina.* Translated by Louise and Aylmer Maude. Ware, UK: Wordsworth, 1999.

Tolstoy, Leo. *The Kreutzer Sonata and Other Stories*. Oxford: Oxford University Press, 2009.

Tolstoy, Count Ilya. *Reminiscences of Tolstoy*. Translated by George Calderon. London: Chapman and Hall, 1914.

Turner, C. J. G. *A Karenina Companion*. Waterloo, Ontario: Wilfrid Laurier University Press, 1993.

Wilson, A. N. *Tolstoy*. London: Atlantic, 2013.

## ON TRANSLATION

Bartlett, Rosamund. "Tolstoy Translated." *Financial Times*, August 8, 2014. https://www.ft.com/content/9cb5c9e0-1e40-11e4-ab52-00144feabdc0#axzz3ADoMiDfk.

Boym, Svetlana. *Common Places: Mythologies of Everyday Life in Russia*. Cambridge, MA: Harvard University Press, 1994.

## ON KATE FIELD AND HER TRAVELS

Cudahy, Brian J. *Under the Sidewalks of New York: The Story of the Greatest Subway System in the World*. New York: Fordham University Press, 1995.

De Leeuw, R. M. *Both Sides of Broadway*. New York: De Leeuw Riehl, 1910.

Field, Kate. *Kate Field's Washington*. 11 vols. 1890–1895.

Field, Kate. *Planchette's Diary*. New York: Redfield Press, 1868.

Field, Kate. *Selected Letters*. Edited by Carolyn J. Moss. Carbondale: Southern Illinois University Press, 1996.

Field, Kate. "On Visiting Pullman." *Kate Field's Washington*, July 11, 1894.

Geberer, Raanan. "The 19th Century's High Line." *Our Town Downtown*, November 17, 2015. https://www.otdowntown.com/news/local-news/the-19th-centurys-high-line-AANP122015111715119920.

Gordon, Sarah Barringer. " 'The Liberty of Self-Degradation': Polygamy, Woman Suffrage, and Consent in Nineteenth-Century America," *The Journal of American History* 83, no. 3 (December 1996): 815–47.

Louden-Brown, Paul. *The White Star Line: An Illustrated History 1869–1934*. UK: Ship Pictorial Productions, 1992.

Marcus, Sharon. *Between Women: Friendship, Desire, and Marriage in Victorian England*. New Jersey: Princeton University Press, 2007.

Reed, Robert C. *The New York Elevated*. South Brunswick, NJ: A. S. Barnes, 1978.

Scharnhorst, Gary. *Kate Field: The Many Lives of a Nineteenth-Century American Journalist*. New York: Syracuse University Press, 2008.

Stamp, Jimmy. "Traveling in Style and Comfort: The Pullman Sleeping Car." Smithsonian.com, December 11, 2013. http://www.smithsonianmag.com/arts-culture/traveling-style-and-comfort-pullman-sleeping-car-180949300/.

White, John H. *The American Railroad Passenger Car*. Baltimore: Johns Hopkins University Press, 1978.

Whiting, Lilian. *Kate Field: A Record*. Boston: Little, Brown, 1899.

## ON ANTHONY TROLLOPE

Glendinning, Victoria. *Anthony Trollope*. New York: Alfred A. Knopf, 1993.

Grennan, Simon. *Dispossession: A Novel of Few Words*. London: Jonathan Cape, 2015.

Trollope, Anthony. *An Autobiography and Other Writings*. Edited by Nicholas Shrimpton. Oxford: Oxford University Press, 2014.

Trollope, Anthony. *Can You Forgive Her?* Edited by Stephen Wall. London: Penguin, 2004.

Trollope, Anthony. *Early Short Stories*. Edited by John Sutherland. Oxford: Oxford University Press, 1994.

Trollope, Anthony. *The Eustace Diamonds*. Edited by Helen Small. Oxford: Oxford University Press, 2011.

Trollope, Anthony. *The Letters of Anthony Trollope*. Edited by N. John Hall. 2 vols. Stanford, CA: Stanford University Press, 1983.

Trollope, Anthony. *The Prime Minister*. Edited by Nicholas Shrimpton. Oxford: Oxford University Press, 2011.

Trollope, Anthony. *The Way We Live Now*. Edited by Francis O'Gorman. Oxford: Oxford University Press, 2016.

## ON STUFF

Byrne, Paula. *The Real Jane Austen: A Life in Small Things*. London: HarperPress, 2013.

Connor, Steven. *Paraphernalia: The Curious Lives of Magical Things*. London: Profile Books, 2011.

Miller, Daniel. *The Comfort of Things*. Cambridge, UK: Polity Press, 2008.

Schor, Naomi. *Reading in Detail: Aesthetics and the Feminine*. London: Routledge, 2007.

## ON TRAINS

Ackroyd, Peter. *London Under*. London: Vintage, 2012.

Attlee, James. *Station to Station: Searching for Stories on the Great Western Line*. London: Guardian Books, 2015.

Bailey, Peter. "Adventures in Space: Victorian Railway Erotics, or Taking Alienation for a Ride." *Journal of Victorian Culture* 9, no. 1 (2004): 1–21.

Bissell, David. "Encountering Stressed Bodies: Slow Creep Transformations and Tipping Points of Commuting Mobilities." *Geoforum* 51 (2014): 191–201.

Brooks, Michael W. *Subway City: Reading the Trains, Reading New York*. New Brunswick, NJ: Rutgers University Press, 1997.

Conrad, Joseph. *The Return*. Edited by Colm Tóibín. London: Hesperus Press, 2014.

Davies, Tony. "Transports of Pleasure: Fiction and Its Audiences in the Later Nineteenth Century" in *Formations of Pleasure*, edited by Fredric Jameson, 45–58. London: Routledge & Kegan Paul, 1983.

Day, John R., and John Reed. *The Story of London's Underground*. London: Capital Transport Publishing, 2010.

Freeman, Michael. *Railways and the Victorian Imagination*. New Haven, CT: Yale University Press, 1999.

Halliday, Stephen. *Underground to Everywhere: London's Underground Railway in the Life of the Capital*. Gloucestershire: History Press, 2013.

Hayles, David. "Pulp Fiction for the Victorian Traveller." *The Times*, July 17, 2010.

*The Kiss in the Tunnel*. 1899. Short silent film. https://player.bfi.org.uk/free /collection/railways-on-film.

Löfgren, Orvar. "Motion and Emotion: Learning to be a Railway Traveller." *Mobilities* 3, no. 3 (2008): 331–51.

MacNeice, Louis. *Autumn Journal*. London: Faber & Faber, 2012.

MacNeice, Louis. "Train to Dublin." In *Collected Poems*, 17–18. London: Faber & Faber, 2007.

Martin, Andrew. *Underground Overground: A Passenger's History of the Tube*. London: Profile Books, 2012.

Nesbit, E. *The Railway Children*. London: Puffin Classics, 2018.

Parissien, Steven. *The English Railway Station*. Swindon, UK: Historic England, 2014.

Schivelbusch, Wolfgang. *The Railway Journey: Trains and Travel in the Nineteenth Century*. New York: Urizen Books, 1979.

Westwood, J. N. *A History of Russian Railways*. London: G. Allen & Unwin, 1964.

Wolmar, Christian. *The Subterranean Railway*. London: Atlantic, 2012.

## ON LOSS, DEATH, AND BEREAVEMENT

Barnes, Julian. *Levels of Life*. London: Vintage, 2014.

Dillon, Brian. *In the Dark Room*. London: Fitzcarraldo Editions, 2018.

Gladwell, Malcolm. *David and Goliath: Underdogs, Misfits and the Art of Battling Giants*. London: Penguin, 2014.

Gross, Kate. *Late Fragments: Everything I Want to Tell You (About this Magnificent Life)*. London: William Collins, 2015.

Hill, Geoffrey. "In Memoriam: Gillian Rose." In *A Treatise of Civil Power*, 35–38. London: Penguin, 2007.

Lucie-Smith, Edward. "The Lesson." In *A Tropical Childhood and Other Poems*, 8. Oxford: Oxford University Press, 1961.

Mannix, Kathryn. *With the End in Mind: Dying, Death, and Wisdom in an Age of Denial*. London: William Collins, 2017.

Mantel, Hilary. *Beyond Black*. London: 4th Estate, 2014.

Miller, David. *Today*. London: Atlantic Books, 2011.

Picardie, Ruth. *Before I Say Goodbye*. London: Penguin, 1998.

Porter, Max. *Grief Is the Thing with Feathers*. London: Faber & Faber, 2015.

Porter, Max. "Kneeling Shepherd." *The Guardian*, January 28, 2017. https://www.theguardian.com/books/2017/jan/28/max-porter-kneeling-shepherd-im-david-miller-saturday-poem.

Roiphe, Katie. *The Violet Hour: Great Writers at the End*. London: Virago, 2016.

Rose, Gillian. *Love's Work*. New York: New York Review of Books Classics, 2011.

Schulz, Kathryn. "When Things Go Missing: Reflections on Two Seasons of Loss." *New Yorker*, February 13, 2017. https://www.newyorker.com/magazine/2017/02/13/when-things-go-missing.

Solnit, Rebecca. *A Field Guide to Getting Lost*. Edinburgh: Canongate, 2017.

Straten, Giorgio van. *In Search of Lost Books: The Forgotten Stories of Eight Mythical Volumes*. London: Pushkin Press, 2017.

Tighe, J. R., and D. R. Davies. *Pathology*. London: Ballière Tindall, 1988.

## ON LOVE AND MARRIAGE

Barnes, Julian. *Flaubert's Parrot*. London: Vintage, 2009.

Cavell, Stanley. *Pursuits of Happiness: The Hollywood Comedy of Remarriage*. Cambridge, MA: Harvard University Press, 1981.

Connolly, Cyril. *Enemies of Promise*. Chicago: University of Chicago Press, 2008.

de Botton, Alain. *Essays in Love*. London: Picador, 2015.

Drabble, Margaret. *A Summer Bird-Cage*. London: Penguin, 1973.

Godwin, Gail. *The Odd Woman*. London: Virago, 2001.

Goethe, Johann Wolfgang von. *Elective Affinities*. Translated by David Constantine. Oxford: Oxford World's Classics, 2008.

Heti, Sheila. *How Should a Person Be?* London: Vintage, 2014.

Knight, India. *In Your Prime: Older, Wiser, Happier*. London: Penguin, 2015.

Knight, India. *My Life on a Plate*. London: Penguin, 2000.

Lurie, Alison, *The War between the Tates*. London: Vintage, 1994.

Penner, Barbara. *Newlyweds on Tour: Honeymooning in Nineteenth-Century America*. Durham: University of New Hampshire Press, 2009.

Perel, Esther. *The State of Affairs: Rethinking Infidelity*. London: Yellow Kite, 2017.

Phillips, Adam. *Monogamy*. London: Faber & Faber, 1996.

Riley, Gwendoline. *First Love*. London: Granta, 2017.

Roiphe, Katie. *In Praise of Messy Lives*. Edinburgh: Canongate Books, 2013.

Tobin, John. *The Honeymoon: A Comedy in Five Acts*. London: David Longworth, 1805.

Updike, John. *Marry Me*. Harmondsworth, UK: Penguin, 1977.

## ON BEING A CHILD, AND ON HAVING AND NOT HAVING CHILDREN

Adébáyò, Ayòbámi. *Stay with Me*. London: Canongate, 2017.

Beauvoir, Simone de. *When Things of the Spirit Come First*. London: Flamingo, 1983.

Binchy, Maeve. "Shepherd's Bush." In *Victoria Line, Central Line*, 217–42. London: Arrow, 2006.

Drabble, Margaret. *The Millstone*. London: Canongate, 2014.

Enright, Anne. *Making Babies: Stumbling into Motherhood*. London: Jonathan Cape, 2004.

Johnson, Barbara. "Apostrophe, Animation, and Abortion." *Diacritics* 16, no. 1 (Spring 1986): 28–47.

Jenkins, Alan. *A Shorter Life*. London: Chatto & Windus, 2005.

Mantel, Hilary. *Giving Up the Ghost: A Memoir*. London: 4th Estate, 2010.

Moran, Caitlin. *How to Be a Woman*. London: Ebury, 2012.

Townsend, Sue. *The Secret Diary and Growing Pains of Adrian Mole aged 13¾*. London: Penguin, 2017.

Wallace, David Foster. "Little Expressionless Animals." In *Girl with Curious Hair*. London: Abacus, 1997.

Ward, Miranda. *Adrift: Fieldnotes on Almost Motherhood*. London: Weidenfeld and Nicolson, 2021.

## ON BAGS

Beckett, Samuel. *Happy Days*. In *The Complete Dramatic Works*, 135–68. London: Faber & Faber, 1986.

Dagognet, François. "Éloge d'un Métaobjet." In *Le Cas du Sac*, edited by Farid Chenoune, 56–61. Paris: Hermès, 2004.

Hiner, Susan. *Accessories to Modernity: Fashion and the Feminine in Nineteenth-Century France*. Philadelphia: University of Pennsylvania Press, 2010.

Jakobson, Roman and Halle, Morris. "The Metaphoric and Metonymic Poles," in *Fundamentals of Language*. Berlin, NY: De Gruyter Mouton, 2002.

Le Guin, Ursula. "The Carrier Bag Theory of Fiction," in *Dancing at the Edge of the World*. London: Grove Press, 1989.

Lurie, Alison. *The Language of Clothes*. New York: Owl Books, 2000.

Ridge, Emily. *Portable Modernisms: The Art of Travelling Light*. Edinburgh: Edinburgh University Press, 2017.

Ropert, Axelle. "12 films, 12 sacs. Une anthologie." In *Le Cas du Sac*, edited by Farid Chenoune, 82–95. Paris: Hermès, 2004.

## ON PHOTOGRAPHY

Barthes, Roland. *Camera Lucida: Reflections on Photography*. Translated by Richard Howard. London: Vintage, 2000.

Bassham, Ben L. *The Theatrical Photographs of Napoleon Sarony*. Ohio: Kent State University Press, 1978.

Berger, John. *Understanding a Photograph*. Edited by Geoff Dyer. London: Penguin, 2013.

Brewer, John. *Out of the Ether: A Wet Plate Collodion Handbook*. John Brewer, 2017.

Calvino, Italo. "The Adventure of a Photographer," in *Difficult Loves*. London: Mariner Books, 1985.

Pauwels, Erin. "Resetting the Camera's Clock: Sarony, Muybridge & the Aesthetics of Wet-Plate Photography." *History and Technology* 31, no. 4 (October 2015): 482–91.

Vestey, Joanna. Afterwords to *Custodians*. Oxford: Ashmolean Museum and Oxford University Press, 2015.

## ON READING

Baker, Nicholson. *U & I: A True Story*. London: Granta, 2001.

Barnes, Julian. *Flaubert's Parrot*. London: Picador, 1984.

Bayard, Pierre. *How to Talk about Books You Haven't Read*. London: Bloomsbury, 2007.

Flint, Kate. "Traveling Readers." In *The Feeling of Reading: Affective Experience and Victorian Literature*, edited by Rachel Ablow, 27–46. Ann Arbor: University of Michigan Press, 2010.

Halpern, Daniel, ed. *Literature as Pleasure*. London: Collins Harvill, 1990.

Mendelson, Edward. *The Things That Matter: What Seven Classic Novels Have to Say about the Stages of Life*. London: Anchor Books, 2007.

Miller, Andy. *The Year of Reading Dangerously: How Fifty Great Books Saved My Life*. London: 4th Estate, 2014.

Smith, Ali. *Artful*. London: Penguin, 2013.

Stewart, Garrett. *The Look of Reading: Book, Painting, Text*. Chicago: University of Chicago Press, 2006.

## ON SPACE AND TIME

Abrahamson, Eric, and David H. Freedman. *A Perfect Mess: The Hidden Benefits of Disorder*. New York: Weidenfeld & Nicolson, 2014.

Bachelard, Gaston. *The Poetics of Space*. London: Penguin, 2014.

Barthes, Roland. *How to Live Together: Novelistic Simulations of Some Everyday Spaces*. Translated by Kate Briggs. New York: Columbia University Press, 2013.

Bowlby, Rachel. *Everyday Stories: The Literary Agenda*. Oxford: Oxford University Press, 2016.

Morson, Gary Saul. *Narrative and Freedom: The Shadows of Time*. New Haven, CT: Yale University Press, 1994.

## ON LIFE WRITING

Cumming, Laura. *The Vanishing Man: In Pursuit of Velázquez*. London: Vintage, 2017.

Feigel, Lara. *Free Woman: Life, Liberation, and Doris Lessing*. London: Bloomsbury Publishing, 2018.

Jefferson, Margo. *Negroland: A Memoir*. London: Granta Books, 2016.

Knausgaard, Karl Ove. *A Death in the Family*. London: Vintage, 2014.

Nelson, Maggie. *The Argonauts*. London: Melville House, 2016.

Schiff, Stacy. *Véra (Mrs. Vladimir Nabokov)*. London: Random House, 1999.

Walsh, Joanna. "On Self-Writing." *Irish Times*, March 31, 2016. https://www.irishtimes.com/culture/books/vertigo-author-joanna-walsh-on-self-writing-1.2592426.

# ACKNOWLEDGMENTS

MUCH OF THIS BOOK IS ABOUT LIFE'S UNEXPECTEDNESS, its chance meetings and route diversions. What follows is an attempt to capture something of that serendipity. I first began to think about Kate Field when I was writing an article about nineteenth-century journalism. While I vaguely knew of Field's existence, it was an anonymous reader who pointed out that Trollope's muse might be worth more than a mention. I am grateful to that reader for illuminating something that was in plain sight, and for starting me thinking. I could not have gone on to imagine, and take liberties with, Kate Field's life without the outstanding works of biographical scholarship by Gary Scharnhorst and Carolyn J. Moss.

Thanks in abundance to:

My wonderful editor, Faith Wilson Stein, for her imagination, kindness, and brilliance. I am also deeply grateful to Anne Gendler, Mary Klein, and to all at Northwestern University Press for all they have done.

To divide up friends and colleagues is invidious, but for those friends first met under the umbrella of academic life, my thanks to Michael Allen, Jonathan Bate, Ushashi Dasgupta, Lara Feigel, Tim Gao, Christine Gerrard, Will Ghosh, Ben Higgins, Lloyd (Meadhbh) Houston, Adrian Poole, and Marion Turner. Thanks and love, in particular, to Helen Barr.

For early readings of fragments, cheer, interest, or for simply giving me the courage to carry on, I am immensely grateful to Ros Ballaster, the late Christopher Butler, Gillian Butler, Charles Chubb, Charles Hulme, Hermione Lee, Lindsay Mackie, Janet Quinn, Sue Potter, Alan Rusbridger, Philippe Sands, Gerry Simpson, Maggie Snowling, Sue Tyson, Bart Van Es, and Kate Womersley. Thanks to Tom Cook, for meticulous comments and insights on draft material, and for generally getting it, and to Edward Mendelson for suggesting, fifteen years ago, that I try reading Trollope.

For completely vital conversations and friendship along the way, thanks and love to Louise Dalton and Tanya Frankel, Amy Shindler and Claudia Fitzgerald. And sorry about that time I killed off a perfectly good evening with an (uninvited) reading from the manuscript at the dinner table.

At different times and in different ways the following people have also inspired or assisted, supported or cheered me. Thank you—Elsa Booth, Paddy and Rebecca Bullard, Richard Butchins, Rachel Buxton, Xander Cansell, Susan Fotherby, Vivienne Gleave, Zoë Hines, Dotti Irving, Stephanie Kelley, Julie Kleeman, Marie Merriman, Frances Neale, Olwen Renowden, David and Jenny Rhymes, Colin Shindler, and Rachael Willis.

For insights into the process of Victorian photography, thanks to John Brewer. For talking about things Russian, Rosamund Bartlett and Anna Benn. For train stuff, thanks to Sam Sheppard. Gratitude to Nancy Browner. Thank you to the Dermatology department of the Churchill Hospital. And, for everything, my thanks to Yvonne Leeds—you've done more than I could ever say to make this all possible.

In Russia, love and buckets of gratitude to the utterly wonderful Anastasia Tolstoy, who took me to her family home at Yasnaya Polyana, to Moscow in search of modern-day Vronskys, and on the night train to St. Petersburg to look for the latter-day Anna Kareninas. Work should always be as much fun as that was. Along the way I was welcomed by Vladimir, Ekaterina, Catherine, and Sergey. Thank you. Thank you to Tom and Fekla for allowing me to crash your Christmas party, interview people about the contents of their bags, and attempt sabrage on a stairwell. Thank you so much, Galina Alexieva and Nadezda Pereverzeva, for your time, intelligence, and care. Galina, for illuminating Tolstoy's reading life. Nadezda, for allowing me to hold Tolstoy's very own copies of Trollope, for explaining what objects meant to Tolstoy, and for finding, as night fell, Sofia's precious handbag. Yuri Savinov and Natalia Shudzeyko got up early on a Sunday morning on the last day of my trip to Russia, and made their way through the snow to allow me to visit the railway carriage museum at Yasenki. Natalia, I am indebted to you for sharing your knowledge of Russian train travel. My thanks to the curators of the Tolstoy Estate Museum in Moscow, and to the costume and props department of Mosfilm.

In London N3, thank you to the owners of my childhood home, for being generous enough to allow me to revisit that space.

To Paula Byrne, who champions the writing of women both past and present, thank you for all your support, friendship, inspiration, and for simply being fabulous.

Thank you thank you to the wonderful Miranda Ward, who followed Kate Field with me, and helped to track down secrets, umbrellas, swans, funerals, photography studios, theater maps, the hidden history of the El train. For astonishing research, subtle brilliance, imagination, friendship, the list goes on . . .

Robert Douglas-Fairhurst, dear and brilliant friend, thank you for reading early scraps, for cocktails, for helping me to imagine that I could even begin to write this.

To my mother and siblings, thanks beyond words. You were generous enough to let me write about the past without asking to read what I said, knowing that mine is only one perspective, and only one version of what happened. Important things I could have said did not have a home in this book. Particularly, the never-ending story I could have written about the love and support you all give me, how much I love you—and the merits of family kitchen-dancing to Finnish YouTube disco videos.

Ivo and Ottilie. You have lived with this book for a very long time. You are wise beyond, and because of, your years. Thank you for being you. I love you to the moon and back, with added fish fingers.

Much gratitude to Arabella Pike and all at William Collins, who got and understood this book from the start, and tended it in its first incarnation. Before that, Peter Straus was good enough to feel I might have something worth saying when we met many years ago, and good enough to want to read it when it finally turned up.

David Miller, all too briefly my agent, was a man who lit up life. He saw what this book might be and, in doing so, helped me to turn my hunch into a book. He died too soon, and too suddenly, in what should have been the middle of his life. I am one of many who miss him still.

Andrew Schuman, my husband named at last—you have done more for this book than I can ever tell you, not least by being its hero. Thank you for the glitter ball. I can only repeat the three words you wrote to me on the back of the taxi receipt in 2011, and I am lucky enough to get to say them every day.

*The last word shall never be said*, according to Conrad, but here goes. This book is dedicated to anyone who has lost too soon.